MW01172925

Rev. Dr. Rod

That Can't Be In The Bible

Vol. 1 of 5

www.revdrrod.org
Ebook & Audio Version Online
freespirit@revdrrod.org

A Computerized Analysis Of
The Holy Scriptures From A
Technical Point Of View

ISBN#
Copyright 2020 # 1-8959026101

The 1st Amendment-Separation
Of Church And State Is A Myth.

The church is governed by the 501-3c tax
exempted status, it mandates that the church
must follow all public related policy to
comply. Whatever is passed into law becomes
public policy and so the church must bow
down in order to remain tax exempt. In reality,
the church is actually bowing to the almighty
dollar. Have you noticed how many churches
have given up the fight against same sex
marriage? It is now public policy and the law
of the land.

Introduction

This book has been written to offer a 21st century analysis of the Holy Scriptures from a technical point of view. By using the latest in computer technology, the bible can now be scanned in seconds, thus giving one the instantaneous power to be able to compare related verses throughout the bible; by doing so, I have discovered several passages in the bible that appear to have been acted out in real life in America, and it's shocking!

Example: The Authorized King James Version Of The Bible 1611, (the bible that America was founded on) teaches that if you do not follow the Four Gospels of Jesus Christ, then you're a heathen (which up until our modern times included all indigenous people and all non-Christians); now read the verses below from the KJV.SRV, about heathens.

Psalms:44:2: How thou didst drive out the heathen with thy hand, and plantedst them; how thou didst afflict the people, and cast them out.

Isn't this exactly what the US. Government, US. Calvary and the American people

(Protestants and Catholics alike) did to the Native American Indians, whom they referred to as "heathen redskins"?

Psalms:18:43: Thou hast delivered me from the strivings of the people; and thou hast made me the head of the heathen: a people whom I have not known shall serve me.

This is why the early Protestants (white Christians) owned slaves in America. Being religious fanatics, they naturally perceived it as their God-given right by what the bible plainly teaches.

King James 1; his court, Westminster Abbey, and all of the college professors at Oxford and Cambridge universities (who participated in the translation of the KJV.-1611) were white supremacists. King James 1, assumed that God had created heaven and earth especially for him and it was his divine right and white privilege to rule (other elites and their subjects followed suit). This white supremacist ideology came to the New World with the founding of the first English colony, Jamestown, Virginia,1607.

The following speech given by Abraham Lincoln in Charleston, Illinois in 1858 (251 years later), depicts the exact attitude that all white Christians shared: "I am not, nor ever have been in favor of bringing about in any way the social and political equality of the white and black races, that I am not, nor ever have been in favor of making voters or jurors of negroes, nor of qualifying them to hold office, nor to intermarry with white people. I as much as any man am in favor of the superior position assigned to the white race."

Assigned by the Authorized King James Version Of The Bible 1611.

If you ask today's Christian to explain the history of their religion the majority of them wouldn't have a clue, and that's just the way the church and Big Brother would like to keep it. Why? Because they know that the bible has influenced followers to take some very weird and bizarre turns in the past and like a skeleton in the closet, the subject is better off left alone, as not to give any other religious fanatic(s) any wild ideas. Besides that, Christianity used to be the catalyst and the church used to be the bond that held America together. Laws were created derived from the KJV.-1611, and the church put the fear of God in people, peer pressure throughout society did the rest.

The purpose of this book is to expose the bible's negative impact on American history and how the scriptures influenced millions of faithful followers into believing that they were a superior race, giving rise to white supremacy and prejudice in America. The root of their hatred and bigotry sprung forth from a seed that was planted in their minds by the scriptures found in the Authorized King James Version Of The Bible 1611; the bible that America was founded on.

Note: The bible verses used in this book have been taken from the KJV. Revised Version, Oxford, 1885, for better comprehension.

Disclaimer: That Can't Be In The Bible By Rev. Dr. Rod is not recommended for minors or anyone who is mentally unstable. The following pages contain barbaric and sadistic literature that maybe harmful to ones mental health and well being. Anyone, who examines the following pages does so at their own risk. Please be advised: The author of this work does not advocate violence, hatred, bashing, racism nor Satanism.

Prepare to be shocked, traumatized, stunned and your world turned upside down, it's your turn to face reality!

Preface

That Can't Be In The Bible began in Big Woods, Louisiana, the center of the Bible Belt, where I lived with my elderly father and stepmother. My stepmother's first two husbands had been Southern Baptist preachers before they died. They were college trained clergymen who left an awesome library in her home of biblical literature and homiletic books (sermon guidelines). To pass the time away and to break the monotony of my serene country life, I began reading through their books. The more I read, the more I began to notice blatant similarities between what was in the bible and what had actually happened in America during its darkest days. I was intrigued by what I read and curious to know if anyone else had ever noticed these similarities. To my knowledge, I had never heard anyone admit that the bible was a negative influence on American history, so I instinctively assumed that there was something mystique about the scriptures that few people were aware of. I began a quest to learn everything that I possibly could about the bible. I became obsessed with the idea and compelled to get to the root of the matter and find out once and for all, what was in the scriptures, and why. Now after studying the bible intensively since 1995 with an open mind, I can clearly understand why it is in the best interest of the church and our government to keep its contents unquestionably obscure; to conceal their misuse of the scriptures! Our American heritage was piece milled together according to what our white Protestant forefathers read in the bible. The scriptures found in the Authorized King James Version Of The Bible 1611, are the basis for our civil law and order and our moral values, though today it's hard to tell. The oppression of women, slavery and even the atrocities committed against the Native American Indians can all be attributed to passages neatly tucked away in the scriptures and that's not all. Americans have used these obscure passages in the bible to justify their crimes against humanity throughout history but today, history is being rewritten and glossed over to conceal their acts of violence, injustice and what influenced them. In fact, the bible has been revised at least five different times since the Civil War ended and it will continue to be revised until all traces of its negative influence are obscure. The Authorized King James Version Of The Bible, is the only resource that one needs to discover the truth about white supremacy, bigotry and injustice, and where it all started.

Unfortunately, America was built on quick sand and it's been sinking ever since! Racial tension is at its highest peak right now with no end in sight (e.g. George Floyd).

About the author: Rev. Dr. Rod is a very patriotic Vietnam veteran, who was ordained in 1997 and was awarded a Doctorate Degree in 2014. He senses the presence of a worldly spirit that he assumes is God; but it has never manifested itself in a physical form, so he can neither explain it, nor describe it.

Our ancestors sensed it too and exploited it by creating mythological theologies about it. They then capitalized on it by forcing their primitive perception of God on the masses.

In other words, if the government is behind

everything you put your faith and trust in brothers and sisters, you're standing on shaky ground!

Note: Certain bible verses used in this book will be encountered more than once, the same is true of the author's point of view that he wants to get across.

If Jesus Died For Our Sins, Then Why Is He Coming Back To Kill Us For Our Sins?

#	Table Of Topics	Pg. #
1	The Grand Illusion	1-13
2	Solving A Biblical Mystery	14-21
3	Bloody Rituals In The Bible	21-32
4	Getting Stoned In The Bible	33-35
5	Mythical Creatures	35-50
6	Christmas Tree	50-52
7	The Oppression Of Women	53-58
8	Burning Babies In the Bible	59-64
9	Getting Drunk In Biblical Times	65-74
10	Thank The Indians	74-79
11	Cannibalism In The Bible	80-82
12	Intercourse	83-86
13	Rape And Incest	87-94
14	Garden Of Eden	95-103
15	Bizarre Verses	104-131
16	Last Days	132-135
17	Closing Statement	136-138

Can You Answer This Question?
The entire bible (scriptures) took place in the middle east and it's an historical record of their customs, culture(s), mythology, perception of God and so on. So why in the world would anybody in their right mind want to establish a country in the western hemisphere such as America, and base it on the same dogmatic principles found in the middle east?

This book exposes the following taboos written about in the Authorized King James Version Of The Bible-RV. 1885; pagan gods and goddesses, sexual perversion, human sacrifice, cannibalism, human mutilation, bloody rituals, curses, spells, potions and witchcraft, rape and incest, animal sacrifices and needles butchery, weird customs, strange stories, bizarre facts and more! Also exposed is the bible's crude and barbaric use of the English language as in the following verses.

Kgs:18:27: But Rab-shakeh said unto them, Hath my master sent me to thy master, and to thee, to speak these words? hath he not sent me to the men which sit on the wall, that they may eat their own dung, and drink their own piss with you.

2Kgs:10:7: And it came to pass, when the letter came to them, that they took the king's sons, and slew seventy persons, and put their heads in baskets, and sent him them to Jezreel.

Hosea:13:16: Samaria shall become desolate; for she hath rebelled against her God: they shall fall by the sword: their infants shall be dashed in pieces, and their women with child shall be ripped up.

Psalms:137:9: Happy shall he be, that taketh and dasheth thy little ones against the stones.

Isa:30:22: Ye shall defile also the covering of thy graven images of silver, and the ornament of thy molten images of gold: thou shalt cast them away as a menstruous cloth; thou shalt say unto it, Get thee hence.

Judg:5:26: She put her hand to the nail, and her right hand to the workmen's hammer; and with the hammer she smote Sisera, she smote off his head, when she had pierced and stricken through his temples.

1Sam:22:19: And Nob, the city of the priests, smote he with the edge of the sword, both men and women, children and sucklings, and oxen, and asses, and sheep, with the edge of the sword.

The following verse was discovered while using a search engine to search the entire bible for every verse that contains the word, fruits.

Ex:22:29: Thou shalt not delay to offer the first of thy ripe fruits, and of thy liquors: the firstborn of thy sons shalt thou give unto me.

Did you notice the word "liquors" in the

verse above? Regardless of how preachers have deliberately tried to misinterpret this passage as being only "grape juice," it's quite obvious what Moses had in mind when he wrote it. The following bible verses also make reference to the use of alcohol.

Prov:31:6: Give strong drink unto him that is ready to perish, and wine unto those that be of heavy hearts.

The following verse points out that wine makes one merry.

Eccl:10:19: A feast is made for laughter, and wine maketh merry: but money answereth all things. The verse below teaches us that there is "no better thing under the sun, than to eat, and to drink, and to be merry."

Eccl:8:15: Then I commended mirth, because a man hath no better thing under the sun, than to eat, and to drink, and to be merry: for that shall abide with him of his labour the days of his life, which God giveth him under the sun.

The next verse, which by the way would be difficult to find without the aid of a search engine tells us that, "Nabal's heart was merry within him, for he was very drunken." So here we learn that when one is "merry," he or she is intoxicated.

1Sam:25:36: And Abigail came to Nabal; and, behold, he held a feast in his house, like the feast of a king; and Nabal's heart was merry within him, for he was very drunken: wherefore she told him nothing, less or more, until the morning light.

The bible verse below is one of my favorites. It plainly states, "and be not drunk with wine wherein is excess; but be filled with the spirit"; or in other words, drink until it makes you feel merry, lovable and happy like Merry Ole England.

Ephesians:5:18: And be not drunk with wine wherein is excess; but be filled with the spirit;

Here it's quite obvious that the bible condones the use of alcohol. However, preachers teach that it should be avoided at all costs like it's one of the Ten Commandments. Preachers have lost the spirit of being merry and instead have taken on an aura of solemnness, that's why followers change churches so often in search of inner peace and happiness.

The bible's negative influence on American history, it's time to stop blaming each other for our racial problems and bigotry, and point our finger instead at the root of our social torment. This book will prove beyond a shadow of a doubt that the bible and its discriminatory and racial message is what caused early white Protestants to mimic its barbaric doctrine in their daily lives.

It doesn't take a master in theology to see that religion has taken some very weird and unusual turns in the past. In his book, Strange Facts About The Bible, Webb Garrison, a biblical scholar claims that the witch hunts that we've all heard about were sparked by the following bible verse.

Exodus:22;18: Thou shalt not suffer a witch to live.

Garrison also claims that men throughout history accepted this verse as a base for ecclesiastical and civil law and that in 1490, Catholic authorities who controlled Europe at the time issued the Malleus Maleficarum, an elaborate textbook for the examination and extermination of witches. Some years later, Garrison claims, Martin Luther (who opposed Catholic views) stated:

"I would have no compassion on the witches. I would burn them all."

If these simple, eight little words: "Thou shalt not suffer a witch to live," had such a profound impact on the mines of those followers who made up the early, white Protestant church, imagine what they thought when they read the following:

Psalms:18:43: Thou hast delivered me from the strivings of the people; and thou hast made me the head of the heathen: a people whom I have not known shall serve me.

Christians throughout history believed that anyone who did not worship Jesus was a heathen (non-Christian/uncircumcised) because that's what the bible teaches. The bible's negative influence on their simple minds lured them into the false perception that they were a superior race. It's critical that you understand that all of the racial prejudice, bigotry and hatred that this country has experienced for over 225 years is the fault of the bible's negative influence on society, and not the fault of its brainwashed followers (white Christians) who were exposed to its cynical doctrine. With this fact as a guidepost, we should all move towards living in harmony with each other and not racially prejudice as the bible teaches.

Lev:25:44: Both thy bondmen, and thy bondmaids, which thou shalt have, shall be of the heathen that are round about you; of them shall ye buy bondmen and bondmaids.

Lev:25:46: And ye shall take them (the heathens) as an inheritance for your children after you, to inherit them for a possession; they shall be your bondmen for ever: but over your brethren the children of Israel, ye shall not rule one over another with rigour.

The African slaves and the Native American Indians were pushed into Christianity by a bulldozer of Christian expansionism that eventually found its way through out the New World, just like it had spread throughout Europe by the bloody, Holy Roman Empire. At the time of the slave trade, African tribesmen and women were worshiping nature and they believed in a vast variety of supernatural spirits; none of which were to be found in the Holy Scriptures. Christians found this appalling and perceived it to be heathen, devil worship which the bible strictly forbids. The verses below were used by Christians to justify owning slaves.

Ex:12:44: But every man's servant that is bought for money, when thou hast circumcised him, then shall he eat thereof.

Gen:17:13: He that is born in thy house, and he that is bought with thy money, must needs be circumcised: and my covenant shall be in your flesh for an everlasting covenant.

Gen:17:23: And Abraham took Ishmael his son, and all that were born in his house, and all that were bought with his money, every male among the men of Abraham's house; and circumcised the flesh of their foreskin in the selfsame day, as God had said unto him.

Gen:17:27: And all the men of his house, born in the house, and bought with money of the stranger, were circumcised with him.

The following verse states that a creditor was going to take a lady's two sons as slaves for money her deceased husband owed, another example of how the bible influenced white Christians in real life to own slaves.

2Kgs:4:1: Now there cried a certain woman of the wives of the sons of the prophets unto Elisha, saying, Thy servant my husband is dead; and thou knowest that thy servant did fear the LORD: and the creditor is come to take unto him my two sons to be bondmen.

Because the Holy Scriptures condone the practice of owning slaves, it was all that white Christians needed to justify bringing African tribesmen and women to America to serve in the fields and other areas of the work force.

The Atrocities Committed Against The Native American Indians (replace the word heathen with the word Indian in the verses below). Protestants And Catholics used the following bible verses to justify slaughtering the Native American Indians, they were taking their cue from what they read in the KJV.-1611.

Psalms:105:44: And gave them the lands of the heathen: and they inherited the labour of the people;

Psalms:44:2: How thou didst drive out the heathen with thy hand, and plantedst them; how thou didst afflict the people, and cast them out.

The bible translators under the authority of King James 1, used at least three different bibles as a guide when they created the Authorized King James Version Of The Bible 1611. I seriously doubt if they had access to the ancient Hebrew text (though they claimed they did).

The first English Bible, written by John Wycliffe, a professor at Oxford university was completed in the late 1300's, at a time when the English language was still in its infancy. This primitive form of English (mixed with Latin) seems more like scribbling
gibberish then cognitive and
coherent writing - as the example below shows.

Wycliffe - Ps:45:7: Hethene men weren disturblid togidere, and rewmes weren bowid doun; God yaf his vois, the erthe was moued.

Wycliffe's use of the word "Hethene" which is an old Germanic term meaning one who lives their life as a nomad, or lives on the plains found it's way into the second English Bible, the Coverdale Bible, as the word "Heithen."

Coverdale – Ps:46:6: The Heithen are madd, the kyngdomes make moch adoo: but whe he sheweth his voyce, ye earth melteth awaye.

In the KJV.-1611, the same word became "heathen" and used to point out anyone who did not worship Jesus Christ. This word was substituted for the word "Gentile" in the Catholic Latin Vulgate Bible ("gentilis"). Gentiles are all non-Jewish people.

This changing of words in the KJV. -1611 had a detrimental effect on the reader's perception and the final out come was devastating for indigenous people the world over!

King Henry, The Eighth, king of England from 1509-1547, loved the Coverdale Bible, as if he had a hand in writing it. I assume that both of them deliberately reworded passages found in the Vulgate Bible as a political conspiracy to justify their own means and ensure the spread of the empire in the New World.

The Catholic,Vulgate Bible was in use for over a thousand years before the Reformation (beginning of the Protestant faith and the circulation of the English Bible).

Below is one of these verses as it appears in the KJV.RV. -1885.

Ps:44:2: How thou didst drive out the heathen with thy hand, and plantedst them; how thou didst afflict the people, and cast them out.

Below is the same verse as it appears in the Douay Rheims Bible; an English version of the much older Catholic, Latin Vulgate Bible from the 4th century.

D.R. - Psalms:43:3: Thy hand destroyed the Gentiles, and thou plantedst them: thou didst afflict the people and cast them out.

Quite a switch, and very effective! Gentiles are all non-Jewish people but it's obvious that they changed the wording (heathens for Gentiles) in Psalms: 44:2, (above) to justify their endeavors in the New World, and to drive out the indigenous people they would encounter. First, the simple minded white colonists, and then in the 19th century, the US. Calvary thought that they were doing the LORD's work but it was all just a political-religious conspiracy previously initiated by the elite white supremacists of Europe. Through imperialism and the bible, the British Empire eventually became one of largest empires the world has ever known and through the English Bible, the English language rapidly spread through out the world. They accomplished what Constantine The Great and the Holy Roman Empire could have only dreamed about.

The KJV., is full of reworded passages taken from the Catholic Bible and it's time to see it for what it really is, a social brainwashing tool, used to enslave the minds of the masses. The traumatic thing about the whole affair is that the KJV-1611, is the bible upon which America was founded. Is it any wonder then that we've been at war with somebody, somewhere in the world for over 250 years, not to mention our own internal, social and racial conflicts?

Who was God talking to when he said, "let us make man in our image, after our likeness"? There have been many theories including one that claims that God was talking to the Holy Trinity, The Father, The Son and The Holy Ghost (Holy Spirit) but that's not what the bible says, that theory's redundant anyway! It's as ludicrous as saying that God was an alien who put stardust in our DNA. It all sounds like mythology to me, not theology but here's what I discovered when I did a computer search of the bible.

According to what's written in the bible; God was not alone in heaven, he was with the host of heaven, whom he had created to be the deities of the Gentiles (non-Jewish people). The host of heaven stand on the right side and on the left side of God, not to mention all the angels that are suppose to be in heaven also. Genesis, the first Book Of Moses contains three mysterious verses that have been puzzling biblical scholars ever since the bible was first published. The first of these mind-boggling verses is encountered in Genesis, Chapter 1, and it has posed to Christendom a biblical mystery puzzle that the average bible totter cannot even begin to piece together, and the third verse can be found in Genesis, Chapter 11.

Gen:11:7: Go to, let us go down, and there confound their language, that they may not understand one another's speech.

These three mysterious verses clearly indicate that God was not alone when he created our known realm of reality. This fact is made obvious when he uses in his statement the pronouns "us" and "our" as he dictates (to someone) what his plans pertaining to man were going to be. What's been puzzling biblical scholars all these years is the unsettling curiosity to know whom God was referring to when he said:

"Let us make man in our image, after our likeness," and, "The man has become as one of us," and, "Let us go down."

Christians like to believe that God was talking to Jesus, or perhaps the angels. However, by using a computer and scanning the entire contents of the scriptures for other verses that shade light on this riddle, I can conclusively prove otherwise. In Genesis, Chapter 2, we're given our first clue as to whom this elusive mystery phantom was.

Gen:2:1: Thus the heavens and the earth were finished, and all the host of them.

Our second clue can be found in the Book Of Nehemiah, Chapter 9:

Neh:9:6: Thou, even thou, art LORD alone; thou hast made heaven, the heaven of heavens, with all their host.

The following verse brings another piece of this mysterious jigsaw puzzle together:

Deu:4:19: And lest thou lift up thine eyes unto heaven, and when thou seest the sun, and moon, and the stars, even all the host of heaven, shouldest thou be driven to worship them, and serve them, which the LORD thy God hath divided unto all the nations under the whole heaven.

From the a fore mentioned verse which was written by Moses (the author of the Torah, the first 5, books of the bible), we can now clearly understand who, and what, these host of heaven are. They're all the other gods and goddesses that have been worshiped in the realm of superstitious, religious fantasy since the beginning of time. Furthermore, according to Moses, God created the host of heaven to be the religious deities of everyone else in the world except for his own chosen people, the Hebrews (the ancient ancestors of the Jews). The following three verses also reinforce and confirm this fact:

Deu:17:3: And hath gone and served other gods, and worshipped them, either the sun, or moon, or any of the host of heaven, which I have not commanded.

Note: These are the words of the Almighty, he is stating that his own chosen people have turned away from worshiping him, and instead have worshiped the host of heaven.

Jere:8:2: And they shall spread them before the sun, and the moon, and all the host of heaven, whom they have loved, and whom they have served, and after whom they have walked, and whom they have sought, and whom they have worshipped: they shall not be gathered, nor buried; they shall be for dung upon the face of the earth.

Jere:19:13: And the houses of Jerusalem,

and the houses of the kings of Judah, shall be defiled as the place of Tophet, because of all the houses upon whose roofs they have burned incense unto all the host of heaven, and poured out drink offerings unto other gods.

I have discovered from reading related verses scattered throughout the bible that the host of heaven stand on the right hand, and on the left hand of the LORD's throne. So obviously, they were there when God said, "Let us make man in our image, after our likeness." Jesus obviously knew this and when asked by the mother of Zebedee's children if her two sons could stand on his right hand and on his left in heaven, Jesus confessed that he did not have the authority to give out these positions. The following verses conclusively substantiates that the host of heaven reside in heaven with God.

1Kings:22:19: And he said, Hear thou therefore the word of the LORD: I saw the LORD sitting on his throne and all the host of heaven standing by him on his right hand and on his left.

Mat:20:23: And he saith unto them, Ye

shall drink indeed of my cup, and be baptized with the baptism that I am baptized with: but to sit on my right hand, and on my left, is not mine to give, but shall be given to them for whom it is prepared of my father.

As previously mentioned, God created the host of heaven and the scriptures themselves make it quite obvious that they're all the other religious deities that have ever been worshiped. So therefore, if you take the bible literally or not, you must now accept the fact that all these host of heaven (numerous gods and goddesses) will be waiting for you in heaven when you die. According to Kings: 22:19, you'll find them standing by God's right hand and on his left. The following verse, the 7th commandment of the Ten Commandments warns the Hebrews against worshiping these host of Heaven.

Deu:5:7: Thou shalt have none other gods before me. Furthermore; it's quite obvious from reading the hidden passages above that God created heaven to be the Home Of The Gods, like Mount Olympus was for the gods and goddesses of Greek mythology. Greek mythology was very well known in the ancient world and it influenced many other belief-systems and sacred texts, the bible being no exception. A simple comparison can easily be made between the Greek mythological legend of Hercules, and that of Samson found in the Book Of Judges; they both possessed super human strength.

So God was not talking to Jesus or the Holy Trinity when he said, "Let us make man in our image, after our likeness." But instead, he was talking to the host of heaven whom he had created and whom he, "hath divided unto all the nations under the whole heaven." The serpent in the Garden Of Eden even knew about the host of heaven when he referred to them while speaking with Eve:

Gen:3:5: For God doth know that in the day ye eat thereof, then your eyes shall be opened, and ye shall be as gods, knowing good and evil.

The gods mentioned in the verse above by the serpent were the host of heaven that God had created; it was not the Trinity, The Father, The Son or The Holy Ghost. Don't you think

that if he really had been talking to his son
Jesus or the Holy Ghost that he surely would
have mentioned it to Moses; after all, Moses
wrote the first five books of the Old Testament
and he never once mentioned the son of God,
the son of man or the name: Jesus.

Just the fact that the bible mentions the
existence of other gods and goddesses casts the
perception that it is nothing more than
mythology itself; a book of fantasy created to
control the minds of the naive through
religious psychosis and theological paranoia.

Bloody Rituals

The bloody rites that were associated with
the ritual and ceremony of the Sacrifice Of
Burnt Offerings in the Old Testament (KJV.
RV.) were macabre to say the least. From what
I've read, I can only hypothesize that the bible
exposes an ancient blood cult that many
Christians aren't even aware of. The following
short story is based on what the Old Testament
tells us about the Sacrifice Of Burnt Offerings.

Imagine yourself being inside a huge tent
with several other people. It's dark outside and

just as dark inside the tent except for a torch that's burning and casting eerie shadows of wavering flames all around you. Beyond the crowd is an altar, it's box shaped and has a large protruding ram's horn extending upward from each of its four corners. As if on cue, the people around you start chanting in an unknown dialect and murmuring in syllables of ecstasy. All of a sudden! There's a violent struggle at the opening of the tent, you quickly turn your head to look and at the same time you try to make the fear that the commotion is causing you subside. You see a man in a ceremonial purple robe forcing a screaming and crying goat into submission. Once the goat's head is firmly wrenched within the man's forearm, he then pulls out a razor sharp, sacred dagger from its sheathe fastened at his waist.

"I offer thee as a burnt offering unto the LORD," the man shouts as he drives the blade deep within the goat's throat and slashes it from ear to ear. Blood starts pumping out of the goat's severed juggler vain with a gurgling death moan and the man in the robe becomes ecstatic as if bewitched by the life that he has just taken.

Another man, also in a purple robe rushes up to the blood gushing carcass of the goat with a large ceremonial urn and as if in a hurry not to waste a single drop of the offering's blood, starts collecting it in the urn; lifting the animal's head over the opening so that the blood flows downward and directly into the base of it. When he gets all the blood that he can force out of the slash in the animal's throat, he then stands upright and holds the ceremonial urn up towards the sky and says,

"Thine offering will make a sweet savour unto thee, oh LORD."

You then see him hurry through the crowd and up to the alter. At the altar, he dips the index finger of his right hand into the ceremonial urn and swirls it around through the animal's freshly drawn blood until it's globed all over his finger. He then raises his hand, as he does the blood rolls back over his wrist and then down his forearm. With a wave of his hand, he then turns and leans over the corner of the alter and begins smearing the warm blood on his finger all over the ram horns.

The people in the ceremony with you begin to get excited as if they anticipate something they've been waiting for about to happen, and they start crowding up closer and closer to the man in the purple robe at the altar. Soon the man in the purple robe finishes his ritual of smearing blood on the ram horns at the altar and then turns and begins pouring the rest of the blood on the floor around its base. As he does; the blood oozes across the floor and smears and splashes as it hits the ground. When he finishes pouring the blood which sanctifies the altar of burnt offerings, he then turns around and starts coming towards the congregation. The people in the crowd began to go into a frenzy as they push by one another trying to be the first one up to the man with the bloody urn. You can't believe what you're seeing!

The man with the ceremonial urn begins sprinkling the remainder of the animal's blood on the people in the congregation; they in turn start smearing it all over each other and acting as if they're in some sort of mind altering trance, or under the spell of some bloody cult leader.

Below are the macabre verses from the KJV. SRV, that inspired me to write the horror story you've just read.

Lev:4:25: And the priest shall take of the blood of the sin offering with his finger, and put it upon the horns of the altar of burnt offering, and shall pour out his blood at the bottom of the altar of burnt offering.

Ex:24:8: And Moses took the blood, and sprinkled it on the people, and said, Behold the blood of the covenant, which the LORD hath made with you concerning all these words.

Heb:9:19: For when Moses had spoken every precept to all the people according to the law, he took the blood of calves and of goats, with water, and scarlet wool, and hyssop, and sprinkled both the book, and all the people,

Ex:29:20: Then shalt thou kill the ram, and take of his blood, and put it upon the tip of the right ear of Aaron, and upon the tip of the right ear of his sons, and upon the thumb of their right hand, and upon the great toe of their right foot, and sprinkle the blood upon the altar round about.

Ex:29:21: And thou shalt take of the blood that is upon the altar, and of the anointing oil, and sprinkle it upon Aaron, and upon his garments, and upon his sons, and upon the garments of his sons with him: and he shall be hallowed, and his garments, and his sons, and his sons' garments with him.

Lev:16:14: And he shall take of the blood of the bullock, and sprinkle it with his finger upon the mercy seat eastward; and before the mercy seat shall he sprinkle of the blood with his finger seven times.

Also included in the bible's bloody rites, a priest would sprinkle some of an animal's blood seven times before the LORD, before the veil of the sanctuary.

Lev: 4:6: And the priest shall dip his finger in the blood, and sprinkle of the blood seven times before the LORD, before the vail of the sanctuary.

Everything that was part of the sacrifice of burnt offerings was sacred. Even the wood had to be from a special tree, and had to be cut and laid upon the fire in a ceremonial fashion as the verse below states:

Lev:1:7: And the sons of Aaron the priest shall put fire upon the altar, and lay the wood in order upon the fire:

Even the animal that was to be sacrificed had to be placed on the alter in a ceremonial fashion:

Lev:1:6: And he shall flay the burnt offering, and cut it into his pieces.

Lev:1:12: And he shall cut it into his pieces, with his head and his fat: and the priest shall lay them in order on the wood that is on the fire which is upon the altar.

Lev:8:20: And he cut the ram into pieces; and Moses burnt the head, and the pieces, and the fat.

It's strange that since God strictly forbid Moses and his people from eating blood that he would insinuate that Israel would eat the flesh and drink the blood of their enemies, whom they would kill in battle.

Num:23:24: Behold, the people shall rise up as a great lion, and lift up himself as a young lion: he shall not lie down until he eat of the prey, and drink the blood of the slain.

Jesus used the same type of metaphor when he said the following.

Jn:6:53: Then Jesus said unto them, Verily, verily, I say unto you, Except ye eat the flesh of the Son of man, and drink his blood, ye have no life in you.

Jn:6:54: Whoso eateth my flesh, and drinketh my blood, hath eternal life; and I will raise him up at the last day.

Jn:6:55: For my flesh is meat indeed, and my blood is drink indeed.

Jn:6:56: He that eateth my flesh, and drinketh my blood, dwelleth in me, and I in him.

One man, Joab, wiped the blood of war on his clothes and also put it in his shoes.

1Kgs:2:5: Moreover thou knowest also what Joab the son of Zeruiah did to me, and what he did to the two captains of the hosts of Israel, unto Abner the son of Ner, and unto Amasa the son of Jether, whom he slew, and shed the blood of war in peace, and put the blood of war upon his girdle that was about his loins, and in his shoes that were on his feet.

Though the sacrificing of animals is

appalling and the constant mention of blood
throughout the bible is disgusting, it gets even
worse as we shall see. Animals were not the
only burnt offerings in the bible. Humans were
sacrificed as well. Judges 11, for example, tells
the story of one man who sacrificed his virgin
daughter (his only child) to the LORD because
he vowed to do so if the LORD helped him
win a war.

Judges:11:30: And Jephthah vowed a vow
unto the LORD, and said, If thou shalt without
fail deliver the children of Ammon into mine
hands,

Judges:11:31: Then it shall be, that
whatsoever cometh forth of the doors of my
house to meet me, when I return in peace from
the children of Ammon, shall surely be the
LORD's, and I will offer it up for a burnt
offering.

Judges:11:34: And Jephthah came to Mizpeh
unto his house, and, behold, his daughter came
out to meet him with timbrels and with dances:
and she was his only child; beside her he had
neither son nor daughter.

Judges:11:35: And it came to pass, when he

saw her, that he rent his clothes, and said, Alas, my daughter! thou hast brought me very low, and thou art one of them that trouble me: for I have opened my mouth unto the LORD, and I cannot go back.

Judges:11:36: And she said unto him, My father, if thou hast opened thy mouth unto the LORD, do to me according to that which hath proceeded out of thy mouth; forasmuch as the LORD hath taken vengeance for thee of thine enemies, even of the children of Ammon.

Judges:11:37: And she said unto her father, Let this thing be done for me: let me alone two months, that I may go up and down upon the mountains, and bewail my virginity, I and my fellows.

Judges:11:38: And he said, Go. And he sent her away for two months: and she went with her companions, and bewailed her virginity upon the mountains.

Judges:11:39: it came to pass at the end of two months, that she returned unto her father, who did with her according to his vow which he had vowed: and she knew no man. And it was a custom in Israel,

Judges:11:40: That the daughters of Israel went yearly to lament the daughter of Jephthah the Gileadite four days in a year.

We all know the story of Abraham, Genesis:22; whom the LORD told to sacrifice his only son, Isaac, as a burnt offering; even though the LORD was only joking, Abraham took him
seriously and proceeded to do it.

Gen:22:2: And he said, Take now thy son, thine only son Isaac, whom thou lovest, and get thee into the land of Moriah; and offer him there for a burnt offering upon one of the mountains which I will tell thee of.

The Authorized King James Version Of The Bible, has been a negative influences on American history for the past 250 plus years; if the Sons Of Liberty in Boston (1773) really wanted to bring about a monumental change, why didn't they throw the bible over board instead of the tea at the Boston Tea Party? It sure would have saved a lot of grief, misery and lives from that day forward. Even today, there are mentally unstable individuals who are influenced by reading the bible and then go off and commit horrific crimes, or they commit unpleasant social disturbances such as passing out biblical literature while trying to save everyone's soul. One thing is for certain, bible societies can't revise the bible fast enough to make a difference and cover its trail of destruction and shame, and negative influence. America is presently in the mist of a social upheaval do to racism and white supremacy, once they become enlightened as to where it all started and whose really to blame (the KJV.-1611) not only will they want to defund the police and tear down confederate statues but there will also be a lot of attention directed at the Authorized King James Version Of The Bible, the white supremacist's handbook!

Note: These mid-eastern psychological tactics were used to drive the masses into religious psychosis and theological paranoia; they served as an example of what to do and what not to do and how one should behave (obey & serve). The bible has been used this way for mind control in America too.

In Genesis 30:14-16: KJV. RV., were told the story of Rachel and the mandrakes. This little story is a very significant one because it plainly states that the ancient ancestors of Jesus used addictive, hallucinogenic substances. Scholars claim that these ancient people only used the mandrakes for their tranquilizing effect and to foster human fertility but regardless of their reason for using them, the fact remains that they got stoned and there's no way to deny it.

Please read the following definition from Webster's Dictionary for the mandrake plant and its compounds then we will examine what roll they played in the Genesis, bible story.

Mandrake: A short-stemmed plant of the nightshade family, Mandragora Officinarum, containing hallucinogenic, narcotic alkaloids.

Nightshade Family: A family of shrubs often containing hallucinogenic alkaloids and narcotic elements such as belladonna.

Alkaloids: An alkaline ring compound common in plants and containing morphine, nicotine, or quinine.

Since ancient times, mandrakes have been

Getting Stoned

sought after for their medicinal properties. The roots of the mandrake plant are very bizarre and grow naturally in the shape of human stick figures. Because of this particularity, charms and amulets have been made from the mandrake roots and all sorts of superstitious, old wives tales have been associated with them. Below are the verses from the bible that show that mandrakes were used in biblical times, thus proving that people in the bible got stoned.

Gen:30:14: And Reuben went in the days of wheat harvest, and found mandrakes in the field, and brought them unto his mother Leah. Then Rachel said to Leah, Give me I pray thee, of thy son's mandrakes.

Gen:30:15: And she said unto her, is it a small matter that thou hast taken my husband? and wouldest thou take away my son's mandrakes also? And Rachel said, therefore he shall lie with thee tonight for thy son's mandrakes.

Gen:30:16: And Jacob came out of the field in the evening, and Leah went out to meet him, and said, Thou must come unto me; for surely I have hired thee with my son's mandrakes. And he lay with her that night.

Rachel wanted to get high on the Mandrakes that Reuben found so bad that she let Leah have her old man for the night. Isn't that called pandering?

The word mandrakes is mentioned again in the Song Of Solomon, which reinforces the popularity of this narcotic plant in biblical times.

Song:7:13: The mandrakes give a smell, and at our gates are all manner of pleasant fruits, new and old, which I have laid up for thee, O my beloved.

Mythical Creatures

Superstition and fantasy have dominated man's thinking ever since he slithered out of the primordial soup and into the rat race. Throughout history, man has used his imagination to explain away things that were beyond his comprehension and even today, man's imagination is running wild causing fantasy to replace reality in every facet of human life. When one reads the bible, one cannot help but be blown away by all the imaginary creatures that the bible talks about, example: unicorns, dragons, satires, etc. Even today, how many people actually believe that the devil is real and that ghosts, angles and demons are a major part of everyday life? There are television shows that come on all hours of the day that sensationalize and exploit these mythological characters and people are gobbling it up and paying to do so. However; whether you agree that the bible should be taken literally or not has no bearing on the fact that up until the 1950's the majority of people certainly did and lived their lives accordingly. In fact, just a few hundred years ago a religious fanatic and psychopath by the name of Cotton Mather, prosecuted over a hundred and fifty women in Salem, Massachusetts for being witches. Superstition is more ingrained in the human psyche than many of us realize, that's one reason why so many people today believe that the bible is to be taken seriously (literally) and that every word in the scriptures is true. The following passages in the bible point out how ludicrous such thinking really is in today's world. Below are verses taken from the bible that dabble in the imaginary realm of make believe and fantasy.

Leviathan:

Job:41:1: Canst thou draw out leviathan with a hook? or his tongue with a cord which thou lettest down?

Ps:74:14: Thou brakest the heads of leviathan in pieces, and gavest him to be meat to the people inhabiting the wilderness.

Ps:104:26: There go the ships: there is that leviathan, whom thou hast made to play therein.

Isa: 27:1: In that day the LORD with his sore and great and strong sword shall punish leviathan the piercing serpent; and he shall slay the dragon that is in the sea.

Leviathan - this legendary sea monster could make the Loc Ness monster look like a tadpole! Legend has it, that it could sallow an entire ship and its crew in one gulp. Legends like this were probably passed down from the Phoenicians, or the Greeks, who were great seafarers (sailors) and who told drunken tales about their voyages at sea to astound young children and other naive listeners.

Unicorn:

Num:23:22: God brought them out of Egypt ; he hath as it were the strength of an unicorn.

Num:24:8: God brought him forth out of Egypt ; he hath as it were the strength of an unicorn: he shall eat up the nations his enemies, and shall break their bones, and pierce them through with his arrows.

Job:39:9: will the unicorn be willing to serve thee, or abide by thy crib?

Job:39:10: Canst thou bind the unicorn with his band in the furrows? or will he harrow the valleys after thee?

Ps:29:6: He maketh them also to skip like a calf; Lebanon and Sirion like a young unicorn.

Ps:92:10: But my horn shalt thou exalt like the horn of an unicorn: I shall be anointed with fresh oil.

Isa:34:7: And the unicorns shall come down with them, and the bullocks with the bulls; and their land shall be soaked with blood, and their dust made fat with fatness.

Unicorn - a mythical creature resembling a

white horse and having a single horn in the center of its forehead. The unicorn was probably incorporated into the bible do to its Grecian influence. The unicorn is as popular today as it ever was.

When the four horsemen in the Book Of Revelation come in the sky to kill us for our sins, each one of them will most-likely be riding a Pegasus, a winged horse that can fly, another mythological creature but not mentioned in the bible by that name.

Satyr:

Isa:34:14: The wild beasts of the desert shall also meet with the wild beast of the island, and the satyr shall cry to his fellow; the screech owl also shall rest there, and find for herself a place of rest.

Isa:13:21: But wild beasts of the desert shall lie there; and their houses shall be full of doleful creatures; and owls shall dwell there, and satyrs shall dance there.

Satyr - a sexual predator of the forest that was part human (from the waist up) and part goat (from the waist down). This creature was very well endowed (sexually) and seduced any young maiden who was foolish enough to wander too far away from her lord and master. The young women were mesmerized and sexually turned-on by the sound of the satyr's flute. The most famous satyr was Pan from Greek & Roman mythology. He was later incorporated into Christian mythology as the devil who supposedly has cloven hooves and horns protruding out of his head.

Cockatrice:

Isa:11:8: And the sucking child shall play on the hole of the asp, and the weaned child shall put his hand on the cockatrice's den.

Isa:14:29: Rejoice not thou, whole Palestina, because the rod of him that smote thee is broken: for out of the serpent's root shall come forth a cockatrice, and his fruit shall be a fiery flying serpent.

Isa:59:5: they hatch cockatrice's eggs, and weave the spider's web: he that eath of their eggs dieth, and that which is crushed breaketh out into a viper.

Cockatrice - a legendary monster with a deadly glance. It had the body of a dragon and the head of a rooster.

Cherub (plural – Cherubim):

Gen:3:24: So he drove out the man;
and he placed at the east of the garden of Eden
Cherubims, and a flaming sword which turned
every way, to keep the way of the tree of life.
2Sam:22:11: And he rode upon a cherub, and
did fly: and he was seen upon the wings of the
wind.

Ps:99:1: The LORD reigneth; let the people
tremble: he sitteth between the cherubims; let
the earth be moved.

Eze:10:8: And there appeared in the
cherubims the form of a man's hand under their
wings.

Cherub - A cherub is a member of the
second order of angels and represented by a
flying, winged baby. Probably incorporated
into Hebrew legend from Greek mythology;
Cupid: Venus' son was a winged baby that flew
around and shot love darts.

Seraphims:

Isa:6:2: Above it stood the seraphims: each
one had six wings; with twain he covered his
face and with twain he covered his feet, and

with twain he did fly.

Isa:6:6: Then flew one of the seraphims unto me, having a live coal in his hand, which he had taken with the tongs from off the altar.

The word Seraphims is only mentioned twice in the bible. It appears to be a name that the author of the Book Of Isaiah, gave to a couple of celestial beings that Isaiah saw in a vision standing above Jehovah, as he sat upon his throne.

Dragon:

Rev:12:3: And there appeared another wonder in heaven; and behold a great red dragon, having seven heads and ten horns and seven crowns upon his heads.

Rev:12:7: And there was war in heaven: Michael and his angels fought against the dragon.

Rev:12:9: And the great dragon was cast out, that old serpent, called the Devil, and Satan, which deceiveth the whole world, was cast out unto the earth.

Dragon - a huge winged reptile, which spits fire and could have one or more heads. In the olden days, the fear of this monster kept small children from wandering too far away from home, like stories of the boogie man scare children today. Probably the legend of the dragon started by the discovery of dinosaur skeletons and or fossils in ancient times.

Wise Serpent, Talking Snake:

Gen:3:1: Now the serpent was more subtle (crafty) than any beast of the field which the LORD God had made. And he said unto the woman, Yea hath God said, Ye shall not eat of every tree of the garden?

Gen:3:4: the serpent said unto the women, Ye shall not surely die.

Gen:3:5: For God doth know that in the day ye eat thereof, then your eyes shall be opened, and ye shall be as gods, knowing good and evil.

Notice Jesus's metaphor in the verse below.

Mt:10:16: Behold, I send you forth as sheep in the midst of wolves: be ye therefore wise as serpents, and harmless as doves.

The Egyptians taught that the serpent symbolized wisdom and Jesus was familiar with the ancient Egyptian Mysteries. Moses made a brazen serpent and put it on a pole, it cured people of poisonous snake bits. It stood for 600 years until around 700 BC. when Hezekiah broke it into pieces during one of his idol smashing binges.

Num:21:8: And the LORD said unto Moses, Make thee a fiery serpent, and set it upon a pole: and it shall come to pass, that every one that is bitten, when he looketh upon it, shall live.

Num:21:9: And Moses made a serpent of brass, and put it upon a pole, and it came to pass, that if a serpent had bitten any man, when he beheld the serpent of brass, he lived.

Smart Ass, Talking Donkey:

Num:22:28: And the LORD opened the mouth of the ass, and she said unto Balaam, what have I done unto thee, that thou hast smitten me these three times?

Num:22:30: And the ass said unto Balaam, Am not I thine ass, upon which thou hast ridden ever since I was thine unto this day? was I ever wont to do so unto thee?

An Ass And A Lion Standing Guard Over A Dead Man:

1Kgs:13:24: And when he was gone, a lion met him by the way, and slew him: and his carcase was cast in the way, and the ass stood by it, the lion also stood by the carcase.

Ghost Writer:

Dan:5:5: In the same hour came forth fingers of a man's hand, and wrote over against the candlestick upon the plaster of the wall of the king's palace: and the king saw the part of the hand that wrote.

Giants:

Gen:6:4: There were giants in the earth in those days; and also after that, when the sons of God came in unto the daughters of men, and they bare children to them, the same became mighty men which were of old, men of renown.

Num:13:33: And there we saw the giants, the sons of Anak, which come of the giants: and we were in our own sight as grasshoppers, and so we were in their sight.

Deut:3:11: For only Og king of Bashan remained of the remnant of giants; behold, his bedstead was a bedstead of iron; is it not in Rabbath of the children of Ammon? nine cubits was the length thereof, and four cubits the breadth of it, after the cubit of a man.

Talking Plants:

Judg:9:14: Then said all the trees unto the bramble, Come thou, and reign over us.

Judg:9:15: And the bramble said unto the trees, If in truth ye anoint me king over you, then come and put your trust in my shadow: and if not, let fire come out of the bramble, and devour the cedars of Lebanon.

Isa:14:8: Yea, the fir trees rejoice at thee, and the cedars of Lebanon, saying, Since thou art laid down, no feller is come up against us.

Singing Trees With Emotions

1Chron:16:33: Then shall the trees of the wood sing out at the presence of the LORD, because he cometh to judge the earth.

Ps:96:12: Let the field be joyful, and all that is therein: then shall all the trees of the wood rejoice.

Ezek:31:9: I have made him fair by the multitude of his branches: so that all the trees of Eden , that were in the garden of God , envied him.

Birds With Voices:

Eccl:12:4: And the doors shall be shut in the streets, when the sound of the grinding is low, and he shall rise up at the voice of the bird, and all the daughters of musick shall be brought low;

Shouting Earth And Singing Mountains:

Isa:44:23: Sing, O ye heavens; for the LORD hath done it: shout, ye lower parts of the earth: break forth into singing, ye mountains, O forest, and every tree therein: for the LORD hath redeemed Jacob, and glorified himself in Israel.

Hand Clapping Trees:

Isa:55:12: For ye shall go out with joy, and be led forth with peace: the mountains and the hills shall break forth before you into singing, and all the trees of the field shall clap their hands.

Fainting Trees:

Ezek:31:15: Thus saith the Lord GOD; In the day when he went down to the grave I caused a mourning: I covered the deep for him, and I restrained the floods thereof, and the great waters were stayed: and I caused

Mythical Creatures

Lebanon to mourn for him, and all the trees of the field fainted for him.

Howling Trees:

Zech:11:2: Howl, fir tree; for the cedar is fallen; because the mighty are spoiled: howl, O ye oaks of Bashan; for the forest of the vintage is come down.

A Good Listener (A Fish):

Jonah:2:10: And the LORD spake unto the fish, and it vomited out Jonah upon the dry land.

Praying Beasts:

Rv:5:14: And the four beasts said, Amen. And the four and twenty elders fell down and worshipped him that liveth for ever and ever.

Talking Devils (Demons/Unclean Spirits):

Mt:8:31: So the devils besought him, saying, If thou cast us out, suffer us to go away into the herd of swine.

Mk:3:11: And unclean spirits, when they saw him, fell down before him, and cried, saying, Thou art the Son of God.

Fowls That Creep On All Four:

Lev:11:20: All fowls that creep, going upon all four, shall be an abomination unto you.

If the "fowls that creep, going upon all four," in the verse above are not some extinct specie of birds, than obviously, it's more biblical fantasy.

Metal Ax Head That Swam:

2Kings:6:44: So he went with them. And when they came to Jordan, they cut down wood.

2Kings:6:45: But as one was felling a beam, the axe head fell into the water: and he cried, and said, Alas, master! for it was borrowed.

2Kings:6:46: And the man of God said, Where fell it? And he shewed him the place. And he cut down a stick, and cast it in thither; and the iron did swim.

2Kings:6:47: Therefore said he, Take it up to thee. And he put out his hand, and took it.

Talking Ribs:

Dan:7:5: And behold another beast, a second, like to a bear, and it raised up itself on one side, and it had three ribs in the mouth of it between the teeth of it: and they said thus unto it, Arise, devour much flesh.

Cloud Shaped Like A Man's Hand:

Mythical Creatures

1Kgs:18:44: And it came to pass at the seventh time, that he said, Behold, there ariseth a little cloud out of the sea, like a man's hand. And he said, Go up, say unto Ahab, Prepare thy chariot, and get thee down, that the rain stop thee not.

A Fish With Money In Its Mouth:

Mt:17:27: Notwithstanding, lest we should offend them, go thou to the sea, and cast an hook, and take up the fish that first cometh up; and when thou hast opened his mouth, thou shalt find a piece of money: that take, and give unto them for me and thee.

This concludes Topic 5 but by no means is it all of the fantasy that can be found in the Authorized King James Version Of The Bible (SRV.).

Christmas Tree

Christmas is without a doubt the most celebrated and commercialized holiday in America. People run themselves into debt every year in order to please their family and friends with special Christmas gifts that are today an established holiday tradition. According to literature freely available, one can discover that the Christmas we celebrate here in America has absolutely nothing to do with Jesus Christ but instead, it is a hodgepodge of pagan-heathen traditions and customs that were woven into Christianity to increase its commercial value and popularity.

In ancient times in the middle east, every culture had its celebrated gods and goddesses. The Roman empire being a world-conquering empire absorbed many of them (they exploited Christianity), so it's not too far fetched to believe that Christianity was concocted out of the most appealing and popular pagan heathen theologies of the day. After all, the only way a government can remain intact and organized is by having its citizens on the same train of thought, religion certainly provides such a catalyst (and that's why America has lost its social bond, religion has taken a backseat when it comes to the mental and physical desires of today's population). Below is what the bible says about having a decorated tree in your

Home.

Jeremiah:10:1: Hear ye the word which the LORD speaketh unto you, O house of Israel:

Jeremiah:10:2: Thus saith the LORD, Learn not the way of the heathen, and be not dismayed at the signs of heaven; for the heathen are dismayed at them.

Jeremiah:10:3: For the customs of the people are vain: for one cutteth a tree out of the forest, the work of the hands of the workman, with the axe.

Jeremiah:10:4: They deck it with silver and with gold; they fasten it with nails and with hammers, that it move not.

The Christmas tree first became popular in Germany in the 1600's; the tradition of putting a decorated tree in the home at Christmas time then came to America via German immigrants, it had never been heard of up until then. American merchants soon realized the sense of enchantment and merriment that having a beautifully decorated Christmas tree can radiate in the home, and their eyes glistened with dollar signs, the rest is history.

Even before 1848, and the advent of the Women's Suffrage Movement, women have been trying to get equal status, equal rights and equal dominance with men. Even today, women are still trying to get the male specie's knee off of their neck. In fact, women didn't even get the right to vote until 1920, with the passage of the 19th Amendment to the Constitution, and that was over 144 years after the country was founded.

Congratulations, sisters on your victory but did you ever wonder why it took so long and why you're still not at the level of social grace that you deserve? Well, as I've said and will continue to say throughout this book; America was founded by God fearing white Christians who took the bible literally. In those days, nothing was accepted as legitimate in society unless it measured up to the biblical standards of the Authorized King James Version Of The Bible-1611 (the bible that America was founded on). The KJV.-1611 is based on the first English Bible, The Coverdale Bible (1535), and that was based on the Catholic Bible (The Vulgate Bible, 4 th century), and that was based on the Torah, the First Five Books Of Moses. The Torah was written in the middle east and God knows how they treat their women, even today!

Let's look now at some verses from the KJV.SRV., and see what it says about women, and how they're to be controlled.

Lev:15:19: And if a woman have an issue, and her issue in her flesh be blood, she shall be put apart seven days: and whosoever toucheth her shall be unclean until the even.

Lev:20:27: A man also or woman that hath a familiar spirit, or that is a wizard, shall surely be put to death: they shall stone them with stones: their blood shall be upon them.

Lev: 21:9: And the daughter of any priest, if she profane herself by playing the whore, she profaneth her father: she shall be burnt with fire.

Lev: 21:14: A widow, or a divorced woman, or profane, or an harlot, these shall he not take: but he shall take a virgin of his own people to wife.

Num:5:27: And when he hath made her to drink the water, then it shall come to pass, that, if she be defiled, and have done trespass against her husband, that the water that causeth the curse shall enter into her, and become bitter, and her belly shall swell, and her thigh shall rot: and the woman shall be a curse among her people.

Num:25:8: And he went after the man of Israel into the tent, and thrust both of them through, the man of Israel, and the woman through her belly. So the plague was stayed from the children of Israel.

Judges:19:29: And when he was come into his house, he took a knife, and laid hold on his concubine, and divided her, together with her bones, into twelve pieces, and sent her into all the coasts of Israel.

Judges:19:25: But the men would not hearken to him: so the man took his concubine, and brought her forth unto them; and they knew her, and abused her all the night until the morning: and when the day began to spring, they let her go.

1 Kings:11:1: And he had seven hundred wives, princesses, and three hundred concubines: and his wives turned away his

heart.

Deu: 23:17: There shall be no whore of the daughters of Israel, nor a sodomite of the sons of Israel.

Romans:7:2: For the woman which hath an husband is bound by the law to her husband so long as he liveth; but if the husband be dead, she is loosed from the law of her husband.

1 Cor:11:7: For a man indeed ought not to cover his head, forasmuch as he is the image and glory of God: but the woman is the glory of the man.

1 Tim:2:11: Let the woman learn in silence with all subjection.

1 Tim:2:12: But I suffer not a woman to teach, nor to usurp authority over the man, but to be in silence.

The verse below teaches married women that their only purpose in life is to please their husbands.

1Cor:7:34: There is difference also between a wife and a virgin. The unmarried woman careth for the things of the Lord, that she may be holy both in body and in spirit: but she that is married careth for the things of the world, how she may please her husband.

The following verse also teaches women to be subservient to their husbands.

Eph:5:23: For the husband is the head of the wife, even as Christ is the head of the church: and he is the saviour of the body.

The verse below clearly indicates through its metaphor that women are of the weaker sex.

1Pt:3:7: Likewise, ye husbands, dwell with them according to knowledge, giving honour unto the wife, as unto the weaker vessel, and as being heirs together of the grace of life; that your prayers be not hindered.

In the first book of the bible (Genesis) you will remember that it was the woman Eve, whose transgression angered the LORD, and caused all humanity to be born into sin. Well, not only did it foul up our lives from birth to death but it also plagued the female gender with a stigma that has tagged them as inferior to men, as-well-as susceptible to temptation. This preordained biblical profile of women, throughout history, has given them an inferiority/guilt complex, that they're still shackled with today.

Job:25:4: How then can man be justified with God? or how can he be clean that is born of a woman?

Prov:31:10: Who can find a virtuous woman? for her price is far above rubies.

Matt:13:38: The field is the world; the good seed are the children of the kingdom; but the tares are the children of the wicked one;

1 John:3:12: Not as Cain, who was of that wicked one, and slew his brother. And wherefore slew he him? Because his own works were evil, and his brother's righteous.

It's quite obvious that the bible's insensitive portrayal of women doesn't fit into today's modern society, that's why it's being revised and glossed over every few years in a desperate attempt to keep it from being phased out completely. I'm really amazed that women didn't have to wear burkas up until they gained their right to vote in 1920.

In the Old Testament, the LORD made many references to various pagan gods and goddesses that were worshiped by his own chosen people during their period of religious confusion, but the one that reigned from hell was Moloch (also called Molech and Chemosh in the scriptures).

Ps:106:37: Yea, they sacrificed their sons and their daughters unto devils,

Deut:12:31: Thou shalt not do so unto the LORD thy God: for every abomination to the LORD, which he hateth, have they done unto their gods; for even their sons and their daughters they have burnt in the fire to their gods.

The following short story is based on what it might have been like to attend an infant sacrifice in the middle east, in biblical times.

Imagine yourself traveling through the desert with a caravan of pagan worshipers. It's pitch black outside and except for the burning torch in the hand of the leader, the only other light being cast is the eerie reflection of the full moon on the rolling sand dunes.

The people around you look strange, the

clothes they're wearing appear to be some sort
of ceremonial garb that reminds you of old
pictures you've seen of medieval circus
performers. Shabby, sun wrinkled old men
move past you puffing on long stemmed pipes
that produce an intoxicating odor, which makes
you even more curious about where the
caravan is heading.

Ahead in the distance, your attention is
drawn to a reddish haze illuminating from
beyond the sand dunes and it adds a sense of
macabre to the dark desert night. Young
women carrying babies, who had been
meandering along behind you, now suddenly
pick up their steps and pass you by; all smiling
and giggling among-st themselves.

As the caravan approaches the crest of a
dune, the sound of hand beaten drums begins
pulsating out a rhythm that awakens a sense of
uneasiness within your soul; your first instinct
is to turn around and go back the way you
came. All of a sudden! One of the young
women carrying a baby grabs your arm and
pulls you along with her as she runs to the top
of the dune. The illuminating reddish haze that

you've been watching becomes brighter and brighter as you get closer to the crest. By now, the others in the caravan ahead of you have started descending down the other side of the dune and are clapping their hands together in some sort of ceremonial rhythm.

At the top of the dune, an intense wave of heat radiates up from the sand and begins to make you sweat and feel uneasy, the girl pulling your arm lets go and runs ahead of you giggling and chanting as she holds her baby overhead. As you gaze out beyond the dunes, you can't believe what you see, perched in the desert is a giant iron statue of a man with a grotesquely, distorted ox head. There are hundreds, if not thousands of pagan worshipers all knelling and chanting in praise to the colossal metal beast. Just then! You see a hooded figure dressed in black, toss a horrified screaming baby unto the flaming cradled palms of the idol.

"Pass through child and become one with Moloch, the god of hell fire," the man shouts as the tender body of the infant convulses, bubbles-down and then disintegrates from the intense heat of the furnace burning within the statue.

Simultaneously, the child's scream turns into a bloody death moan as its life is taken away and its spirit passes through the fire to Moloch.

The crowd goes into a frenzy and the cheers of celebration combined with the ceremonial drums can be heard echoing throughout the night; while the smell of burning flesh and smoke drifts over head.

How did the worship of Moloch and the burning of babies begin? Though the bible claims that Sodom and Gomorrah were both destroyed by God with fire and brimstone for their evil ways, another version of the story can be pieced together by analyzing the scriptures themselves.

The only survivors from the destruction of Sodom and Gomorrah were Lot and his two daughters.
The daughters soon had children by their father, who's names were Moab and Ammon. In the following verses we can see that it is their descendants who engaged in the worship

of the idol Molech, and or Moloch.

1Kings:11:7, Then did Solomon build an high place for Chemosh, the abomination of Moab, in the hill that is before Jerusalem, and for Molech, the abomination of the children of Ammon.

2Kings:17:17, And they caused their sons and their daughters to pass through the fire to Moloch.

This brings to mind, two profound questions that need to be clarified.

(1) If Sodom and Gomorrah really were destroyed by God with fire and brimstone, why wouldn't Lot have brought his two sons: Moab and Ammon up worshiping Jehovah, after-all, it was the angels of the LORD who warned Lot to flee to the mountains in the first place? And it seems that a strict devotion to Jehovah would have been a natural turn of events throughout the rest of biblical history.

(2) Why did the descendants of Moab and Ammon worship Moloch, unless the destruction of Sodom and Gomorrah actually occurred do to some natural disaster (volcanic perhaps or a meteor) that was perceived by

Pg. 64   Burning Babies

those ancient people as a curse from the ruler
of the underworld? The worship of Moloch
was nothing-more-than heathen devil worship!
His sacrificial rites included the sacrificing of
human babies, who were tossed alive onto a
brazen alter, heated to an intense, red hot glow.
The barbaric ideology behind this was that the
spirit of the underworld would grant special
favors and protection to parents who offered
their babies as a sacrifice. This type of
primitive barbarism has been duplicated the
world over by our ignorant monkey minded
ancestors. Who assumed that nature had
intelligence and a personality that they could
manipulate to get what they wanted. Just by
putting such horrific accounts of burning
babies in the bible tells me that the authors of
the bible weren't too much wiser then the brain
dead middle easterners who committed such
atrocities!

Like every other principle we learn from the scriptures, one can always find two sides to a lesson, one that forbids a particular incident and then another verse that condones it. This is how the bible has blended in so well with society for all these years. However, since the Civil War, the scriptures have had difficulty keeping up with man's expanding consciousness and so there has been an essential need to revise the bible, this has been done more than five times in the past 150 years. Bible societies usually want to branch out and perhaps create a new denomination of the Protestant faith, and like their predecessors, they want their own bible (one that's glossed over and sugar coated).

We all know that alcohol and religion don't mix, right, well then, what is the following verse doing in the bible?

Ephesians:5:18: And be not drunk with wine wherein is excess; but be filled with the spirit.

It's no secret that the clergy has tried to convince their followers that the wine mentioned in the bible was only grape juice. Hence, "fruit of the vine" but after reading all of the verses in the bible that pertain to wine and especially drunkenness, I think they're in denial. If you remember, Jesus's first miracle was to turn six jugs of water into wine at the biding of his own mother, Mary? The following two verses convey what was said about the quality of that wine.

Jn:2:9: When the ruler of the feast had tasted the water that was made wine, and knew not whence it was: (but the servants which drew the water knew;) the governor of the feast called the bridegroom.

Jn:2:10: And saith unto him, Every man at the beginning doth set forth good wine; and when men have well drunk, then that which is worse: but thou hast kept the good wine until now.

The following verses in the Gospel of Luke, is what Jesus said about wine.

Luke:5:37: And no man putteth new wine into old bottles; else the new wine will burst the bottles, and be spilled, and the bottles shall perish.

Luke:5:38: But new wine must be put into new bottles; and both are preserved.

Luke:5:39: No man also having drunk old wine straightway desireth new: for he saith, The old is better.

From the three verses above: What do you suppose would make the old bottles burst? Could it be the pressure from the gas that is released during fermentation (alcohol fermentation)? Also, does grape juice change in flavor over time? I know wine does as it ferments and produces more alcohol. Is it wine, or is it grape juice? The verses below can only be interpreted one way, see for yourself.

Exodus:22:29: Thou shalt not delay to offer the first of thy ripe fruits, and of thy best liquors.

Jere:35:2: bring them into the house of the LORD, and give them wine to drink,

1Tim:5:23: Drink no longer water, but use a little wine for thy stomach's sake and thine often infirmities.

Proverbs:31:6: Give strong drink unto him that is ready to perish, and wine unto those that be of heavy heart.

Jere:13:12: Thus saith the LORD God, every bottle shall be filled with wine.

Zech:9:17: corn shall make the young man cheerful, and new wine the maids.

Zech:10:7: and their hearts shall rejoice with good wine.

Ecc:9:7: go thy way and eat thy bread with joy and drink thy wine with a merry heart.

Matt:26:29: But I say unto you, I will not drink hence forth of this fruit of the vine, until the day when I drink it new with you in my father's kingdom.

Luke:7:34: The Son of man is coming eating and drinking; and ye say, Behold a gluttonous man, and a winebibbler.

Pslams:104:15: Wine maketh glad the heart of man.

Ecc:1:10:19: A feast is made for laughter, and wine maketh merry: but money answereth all things.

Ecc:8:15: A man hath no better thing under the sun, than to eat, to drink and to be merry.

1Sam:25:36: And Abigail came to Nabal; and, behold, he held a feast in his house, like the feast of a king; and Nabal's heart was merry within him, for he was very drunken: wherefore she told him nothing, less or more, until the morning light.

Gen:9:21: And he drank of the wine, and was drunken; and he was uncovered within his tent.

Deut:21:20: And they shall say unto the elders of his city, This our son is stubborn and rebellious, he will not obey our voice; he is a glutton, and a drunkard.

1Sam:1:13: Now Hannah, she spake in her heart; only her lips moved, but her voice was not heard: therefore Eli thought she had been drunken.

1Sam:1:14: And Eli said unto her, How long wilt thou be drunken? put away thy wine from thee.

1Kgs:16:9: And his servant Zimri, captain of half his chariots, conspired against him, as he was in Tirzah, drinking himself drunk in the house of Arza steward of his house in Tirzah.

1Kgs:20:16: And they went out at noon. But Ben-hadad was drinking himself drunk in the pavilions, he and the kings, the thirty and two kings that helped him.

Job:12:25: They grope in the dark without light, and he maketh them to stagger like a drunken man.

1Sam:1:13: Now Hannah, she spake in her heart; only her lips moved, but her voice was not heard: therefore Eli thought she had been drunken.

1Sam:1:14: And Eli said unto her, How long wilt thou be drunken? put away thy wine from thee.

1Kgs:20:16: And they went out at noon. But Ben-hadad was drinking himself drunk in the pavilions, he and the kings, the thirty and two kings that helped him.

Job:12:25: They grope in the dark without light, and he maketh them to stagger like a drunken man.

Ps:107:27: They reel to and fro, and stagger like a drunken man, and are at their wits' end.

Prov:23:21: For the drunkard and the glutton shall come to poverty: and drowsiness shall clothe a man with rags.

Prov:26:9: As a thorn goeth up into the hand of a drunkard, so is a parable in the mouth of fools.

Isa:19:14: The LORD hath mingled a perverse spirit in the midst thereof: and they have caused Egypt to err in every work thereof, as a drunken man staggereth in his vomit.

Ps:69:12: They that sit in the gate speak against me; and I was the song of the drunkards.

Isa:24:20: The earth shall reel to and fro like a drunkard, and shall be removed like a cottage; and the transgression thereof shall be heavy upon it; and it shall fall, and not rise again.

Isa:29:9: Stay yourselves, and wonder; cry ye out, and cry: they are drunken, but not with wine; they stagger, but not with strong drink.

Isa:49:26: And I will feed them that oppress thee with their own flesh; and they shall be drunken with their own blood, as with sweet wine: and all flesh shall know that I the LORD am thy Saviour and thy Redeemer, the mighty One of Jacob.

Isa:51:21: Therefore hear now this, thou afflicted, and drunken, but not with wine:

Isa:63:6: And I will tread down the people in mine anger, and make them drunk in my fury, and I will bring down their strength to the earth.

Getting Drunk

Jer:13:13: Then shalt thou say unto them, Thus saith the LORD, Behold, I will fill all the inhabitants of this land, even the kings that sit upon David's throne, and the priests, and the prophets, and all the inhabitants of Jerusalem, with drunkenness.

Jer:23:9: Mine heart within me is broken because of the prophets; all my bones shake; I am like a drunken man, and like a man whom wine hath overcome, because of the LORD, and because of the words of his holiness.

Jer:25:27: Therefore thou shalt say unto them, Thus saith the LORD of hosts, the God of Israel; Drink ye, and be drunken, and spue, and fall, and rise no more, because of the sword which I will send among you.

Jer:48:26: Make ye him drunken: for he magnified himself against the LORD: Moab also shall wallow in his vomit, and he also shall be in derision.

Jer:51:7: Babylon hath been a golden cup in the LORD's hand, that made all the earth drunken: the nations have drunken of her wine; therefore the nations are mad.

Jer:51:39: In their heat I will make their

feasts, and I will make them drunken, that they may rejoice, and sleep a perpetual sleep, and not wake, saith the LORD.

Jer:51:57: And I will make drunk her princes, and her wise men, her captains, and her rulers, and her mighty men: and they shall sleep a perpetual sleep, and not wake, saith the King, whose name is the LORD of hosts.

Lam:3:15: He hath filled me with bitterness, he hath made me drunken with wormwood.

Lam:4:21: Rejoice and be glad, O daughter of Edom, that dwellest in the land of Uz; the cup also shall pass through unto thee: thou shalt be drunken, and shalt make thyself naked.

Joel:1:5: Awake, ye drunkards, and weep; and howl, all ye drinkers of wine, because of the new wine; for it is cut off from your mouth.

Nahum:1:10: For while they be folden together as thorns, and while they are drunken as drunkards, they shall be devoured as stubble fully dry.

Nahum:3:11: Thou also shalt be drunken: thou shalt be hid, thou also shalt seek strength because of the enemy.

Hab:2:15: Woe unto him that giveth his

neighbour drink, that puttest thy bottle to him, and makest him drunken also, that thou mayest look on their nakedness!

Thank The Indians

Every year people in America celebrate Thanksgiving and it brings to mind the story of the Pilgrims, who would have starved to death their first winter if the local Indians hadn't shared their corn with them. Corn is a native plant of the Americas and grew nowhere else until European explorers shipped it back home as one of their marvelous discoveries from the New World.

Today, corn is one of the most widely consumed sources of food and the entire world owes it all to the generosity of the Native American Indians. However, when one reads the bible, one can find ninety-five separate references to corn in the King James Version Of The Bible RV. It's even written about in the Douay Rheims Bible, the English translation of the Catholic Bible. What boggles my mind is, why is corn mentioned in the bible at all? Bible scholars who fear damnation and defend the scriptures at all cost and by any means necessary claim that the name "corn" was given to several different varieties of field crops, and any mention of it in the bible is only giving reference to millet or spelt, common cereal crops known to the people of the middle east. Below is the only verse in the bible that mentions the word "millet." The word "spelt" is not even mentioned in the bible. From the verse below, we can see that when the English translators of the bible used the word "millet" they were talking about an entirely different crop than the corn that the Indians gave to the Pilgrims that first winter; otherwise, they would have used the word "corn" instead of the word "millet," in the verse.

Ezek:4:9: Take thou also unto thee wheat, and barley, and beans, and lentiles, and millet, and fitches, and put them in one vessel, and make thee bread thereof, according to the number of the days that thou shalt lie upon thy side, three hundred and ninety days shalt thou eat thereof.

In my humble opinion, I speculate that the

translators of the KJV.-1611, added their newly discovered treat "corn" to the bible to boost its popularity, and to hype-up the excitement and intrigue of exploring and colonizing the New World. The New World was at the top of England's colonization list around the same time that the KJV.-1611, was being created in 1604, in 1607, England established its first colony in the New World at Jamestown, Virginia. In 1611, the KJV.-1611, was published and King James 1, gave the order that it was to be the only bible allowed in the colony.

The English translators of the King James Version Of The Bible-1611, had a political motive for creating their own translation of the scriptures, plus, they were in fierce competition with the Catholics (who already had their own bible) to conquer the world (or what they could acquire of it). By including verses pertaining to "corn" in the KJV.-1611 (especially in relationship to Jesus) created the illusion that the New World was the biblical equivalent of the Promised Land.

I did some research on the field crops, millet and spelt and neither one of them would make a good bowl of cornflakes, if so, they would have been eating them in the middle east long before John Kelloggs produced them in America in 1878. Let's look now at what Jesus supposedly said about "corn."

Mark:4:28: "For the earth bringeth forth fruit of herself; first the blade, then the ear, after that the full corn in the ear."

If that's not an exact description of Native American, Indian corn, then I'll stop eating cornbread!

In the Gospel of Matthew, we read that Jesus walked through a corn field on the sabbath day, strictly forbidden by the Law Of Moses.

Mat:12:1: At that time Jesus went on the sabbath day through the corn: and his disciples were an hungred, and began to pluck the ears of corn, and to eat it.

Here, I would like to make a comparison between what Jesus and his disciples did on the sabbath and what another man did, it will also give you a peek into:

That Can't Be In The Bible- Vol. 2.

Ex:35:2: Six days shall work be done, but on the seventh day there shall be to you an holy day, a sabbath of rest to the LORD: whosoever doeth work therein shall be put to death.

Moses even ordered one man stoned to death because he gathered sticks for firewood on the sabbath.

Num:15:32: And while the children of Israel were in the wilderness, they found a man that gathered sticks upon the sabbath day.

Num:15:33: And they that found him gathering sticks brought him unto Moses and Aaron, and unto all the congregation.

Num:15:35: And the LORD said unto Moses, The man shall be surely put to death: all the congregation shall stone him with stones without the camp.

Num:15:36: And all the congregation brought him without the camp, and stoned him with stones, and he died; as the LORD commanded Moses.

A person could have been put to death for doing anything unlawful on the Sabbath day.

Jesus knew that, yet he and his disciples did whatever they wanted to on the Sabbath, making a total mockery of the Law Of Moses.

Perhaps the next revision of the bible will clarify this misconception and mention the fact that it was the Indians of North America, who introduced "corn" to the outside world, and the "corn" that is so popular today was virtually nonexistent outside of the Americas and especially in the middle east, where the bible comes from.

Author's note: The Patuxet tribe of Native American Indians who saved the Pilgrims (Christian Separatists) from starving to death that miserable, first winter, were wiped out within 50 years. Historians claim it was from a plaque, Right! The Aztecs, in what is now Mexico were wiped out by a plaque too, just after Hernan Cortes and his bloody band of conquistadors (Catholics) conquered them. In those days, where ever the bible went, the indigenous people were annihilated, so let's drop the excuses and stop making up history as we go along. Shall we?

Cannibalism

The verses below whether used as a metaphor or not are so out of touch with our sophisticated society that it appears as if they had been written by Edgar Allen Poe. Just the same; in some cases, the people in the ancient middle east really did have to resort to cannibalism. This happened when they were besieged in battle by an enemy or during times of great famine. The following three verses imply that this is exactly what happened.

Deut:28:53: And thou shalt eat the fruit of thine own body, the flesh of thy sons and of thy daughters, which the LORD thy God hath given thee, in the siege, and in the straitness, wherewith thine enemies shall distress thee: 2 Kings: 6:28: And the king said unto her, What aileth thee? And she answered, This woman said unto me, Give thy son, that we may eat him to day, and we will eat my son tomorrow.

2 Kings 6:29: So we boiled my son, and did eat him: and I said unto her on the next day, Give thy son, that we may eat him: and she hath hid her son.

The next verse points out how desperate

people were during a siege. They had to resort to eating bird crap and donkey heads.

2Kgs:6:25: And there was a great famine in Samaria: and, behold, they besieged it, until an ass's head was sold for fourscore pieces of silver, and the fourth part of a cab of dove's dung for five pieces of silver.

Below are a few more examples of eating human flesh.

Ezek:5:10: Therefore the fathers shall eat the sons in the midst of thee, and the sons shall eat their fathers; and I will execute judgments in thee, and the whole remnant of thee will I scatter into all the winds.

Zech:11:9: Then said I, I will not feed you: that that dieth, let it die; and that that is to be cut off, let it be cut off; and let the rest eat every one the flesh of another.

Micah:3:3: Who also eat the flesh of my people, and flay their skin from off them; and they break their bones, and chop them in pieces, as for the pot, and as flesh within the caldron.

Rv:19:18: That ye may eat the flesh of

kings, and the flesh of captains, and the flesh of mighty men, and the flesh of horses, and of them that sit on them, and the flesh of all men, both free and bond, both small and great.

The last two verses (surprisingly enough) are the words of Jesus. It was metaphors like these that he made which cost him his life for breaking the Law of Moses. More will be said about Jesus and how he could not or would not follow the Law Of Moses in:

That Can't Be In The Bible Vol. 2

Jn:6:54: Whoso eateth my flesh, and drinketh my blood, hath eternal life; and I will raise him up at the last day.

Jn:6:55: For my flesh is meat indeed, and my blood is drink indeed.

Here's something to think about: God gave Moses the Law; why would the all knowing God give Moses Laws that his son Jesus, could not or would not follow which cost him his life, at the age of 33 years old?

The bible has its own way of referring to sexual intercourse and it points out the act of making love in simplistic literary phrases; "lie with," "go in unto," or "know." We will now examine a few of the verses in the bible that refer to this natural act of human pleasure.

Gen:19:32: Come, let us make our father drink wine, and we will lie with him, that we may preserve seed of our father.

Gen:19:34: And it came to pass on the morrow, that the firstborn said unto the younger, Behold, I lay yesternight with my father: let us make him drink wine this night also; and go thou in, and lie with him, that we may preserve seed of our Father.

Gen:30:15: And she said unto her, Is it a small matter that thou hast taken my husband? and wouldest thou take away my son's mandrakes also? And Rachel said, Therefore he shall lie with thee to night for thy son's mandrakes.

Gen:39:14: That she called unto the men of her house, and spake unto them, saying, See, he hath brought in an Hebrew unto us to mock us; he came in unto me to lie with me, and I cried with a loud voice:

Ex:22:16: And if a man entice a maid that is not betrothed, and lie with her, he shall surely endow her to be his wife.

Lev:15:18: The woman also with whom man shall lie with seed of copulation, they shall both bathe themselves in water, and be unclean until the even.

Lev:15:24: And if any man lie with her at all, and her flowers be upon him, he shall be unclean seven days; and all the bed whereon he lieth shall be unclean.

Lev:18:22: Thou shalt not lie with mankind, as with womankind: it is abomination.

Lev:18:23: Neither shalt thou lie with any beast to defile thyself therewith: neither shall any woman stand before a beast to lie down thereto: it is confusion.

Lev:20:12: And if a man lie with his daughter in law, both of them shall surely be put to death: they have wrought confusion; their blood shall be upon them.

Lev:20:13: If a man also lie with mankind, as he lieth with a woman, both of them have committed an abomination: they shall surely be put to death; their blood shall be upon them.

Lev:20:15: And if a man lie with a beast, he shall surely be put to death: and ye shall slay the beast.

Lev:20:18: And if a man shall lie with a woman having her sickness, and shall uncover her nakedness; he hath discovered her fountain, and she hath uncovered the fountain of her blood: and both of them shall be cut off from among their people.

Lev:20:20: And if a man shall lie with his uncle's wife, he hath uncovered his uncle's nakedness: they shall bear their sin; they shall die childless.

Num:5:13: And a man lie with her carnally, and it be hid from the eyes of her husband, and be kept close, and she be defiled, and there be no witness against her, neither she be taken with the manner;

Deut:22:23: If a damsel that is a virgin be betrothed unto an husband, and a man find her in the city, and lie with her;

2Sam:12:11: Thus saith the LORD, Behold, I will raise up evil against thee out of thine own house, and I will take thy wives before thine eyes, and give them unto thy neighbour, and he shall lie with thy wives in the sight of this sun.

2Sam:13:11: And when she had brought them unto him to eat, he took hold of her, and said unto her, Come lie with me, my sister.

Gen:16:2: And Sarai said unto Abram, Behold now, the LORD hath restrained me from bearing: I pray thee, go in unto my maid; it may be that I may obtain children by her. And Abram hearkened to the voice of Sarai.

Gen:29:21: And Jacob said unto Laban, Give me my wife, for my days are fulfilled, that I may go in unto her.

Gen:30:3: And she said, Behold my maid Bilhah, go in unto her; and she shall bear upon my knees that I may also have children by her.

The bible story below depicts a shocking account of how one man, Amnon, raped his own sister. Amnon was later killed for his evil deed when his brother Absalom, ordered his servants to slay him. (Note: More fables from the middle east).

2 Samuel:13:2-14.

1: And it came to pass after this, that Absalom the son of David had a fair sister, whose name was Tamar; and Amnon the son of David loved her.

2: And Amnon was so vexed, that he fell sick for his sister Tamar; for she was a virgin; and Amnon thought it hard for him to do any thing to her.

3: But Amnon had a friend, whose name was Jonadab, the son of Shimeah David's brother: and Jonadab was a very subtil man.

4: And he said unto him, Why art thou, being the king's son, lean from day to day? wilt thou not tell me? And Amnon said unto him, I love Tamar, my brother Absalom's sister.

5: And Jonadab said unto him, Lay thee down on thy bed, and make thyself sick: and when thy father cometh to see thee, say unto him, I pray thee, let my sister Tamar come, and give me meat, and dress the meat in my sight, that I may see it, and eat it at her hand.

6: So Amnon lay down, and made himself sick: and when the king was come to see him, Amnon said unto the king, I pray thee, let Tamar my sister come, and make me a couple of cakes in my sight, that I may eat at her hand.

7: Then David sent home to Tamar, saying, Go now to thy brother Amnon's house, and dress him meat.

8: So Tamar went to her brother Amnon's house; and he was laid down. And she took flour, and kneaded it, and made cakes in his sight, and did bake the cakes.

9: And she took a pan, and poured them out before him; but he refused to eat. And Amnon said, Have out all men from me. And they went out every man from him.

10: And Amnon said unto Tamar, Bring the meat into the chamber, that I may eat of thine hand. And Tamar took the cakes which she had made, and brought them into the chamber to Amnon her brother.

11: And when she had brought them unto him to eat, he took hold of her, and said unto her, Come lie with me, my sister.

12: And she answered him, Nay, my brother, do not force me; for no such thing ought to be done in Israel: do not thou this folly.

14: Howbeit he would not hearken unto her voice: but, being stronger than she, forced her, and lay with her.

Incest In The Bible

The following incident of incest in the bible happened just after the destruction of Sodom and Gomorrah, when Lot's own two daughters raped him after getting him drunk on wine.

Gen:19:30-38.

30: And Lot went up out of Zoar, and dwelt in the mountain, and his two daughters with him; for he feared to dwell in Zoar: and he dwelt in a cave, he and his two daughters.

31: And the firstborn said unto the younger, Our father is old, and there is not a man in the earth to come in unto us after the manner of all the earth:

32: Come, let us make our father drink wine, and we will lie with him, that we may preserve seed of our father.

33: And they made their father drink wine that night: and the firstborn went in, and lay with her father; and he perceived not when she lay down, nor when she arose.

34: And it came to pass on the morrow, that the firstborn said unto the younger, Behold, I lay yesternight with my father: let us make him drink wine this night also; and go thou in, and lie with him, that we may preserve seed of our Father.

35: And they made their father drink wine that night also: and the younger arose, and lay with him; and he perceived not when she lay down, nor when she arose.

36: Thus were both the daughters of Lot with child by their father.

37: And the firstborn bare a son, and called his name Moab: the same is the father of the Moabites unto this day.

38: And the younger, she also bare a son, and called his name Benammi: the same is the father of the children of Ammon unto this day.

Another act of incest in the bible that we will examine is when Abraham, apparently married his own half-sister, as stated by Moses.

Gen:20:12: And yet indeed she is my sister; she is the daughter of my father, but not the daughter of my mother; and she became my wife.

The next case of incest in question, is when Nahor took his brother's daughter, his own niece, as a wife.

Gen:27-29.

27: Now these are the generations of Terah: Terah begat Abram, Nahor, and Haran; and Haran begat Lot.

28: And Haran died before his father Terah in the land of his nativity, in Ur of the Chaldees.

29: And Abram and Nahor took them wives: the name of Abram's wife was Sarai; and the name of Nahor's wife, Milcah, the daughter of Haran, the father of Milcah, and the father of Iscah.

Another case of incest in the bible that is most interesting is stated in Exodus:6:20, where it points out that Moses's own mother was actually his aunt too.

Ex:6:20: And Amram took him Jochebed his

father's sister to wife; and she bare him Aaron and Moses: and the years of the life of Amram were an hundred and thirty and seven years.

The next case of incest that we will examine is the amusing story of how Judah's daughter in-law pretended to be a prostitute, so that she could get pregnant by her deceased husband's father.

Gen:38:13-27.

13: And it was told Tamar, saying, Behold thy father in law goeth up to Timnath to shear his sheep.

14: And she put her widow's garments off from her, and covered her with a vail, and wrapped herself, and sat in an open place, which is by the way to Timnath; for she saw that Shelah was grown, and she was not given unto him to wife.

15: When Judah saw her, he thought her to be an harlot; because she had covered her face.

16: And he turned unto her by the way, and said, Go to, I pray thee, let me come in unto thee; (for he knew not that she was his daughter in law.) And she said,

What wilt thou give me, that thou mayest come in unto me?

17: And he said, I will send thee a kid from the flock. And she said, Wilt thou give me a pledge, till thou send it?

18: And he said, What pledge shall I give thee? And she said, Thy signet, and thy bracelets, and thy staff that is in thine hand. And he gave it her, and came in unto her, and she conceived by him.

19: And she arose, and went away, and laid by her vail from her, and put on the garments of her widowhood.

20: And Judah sent the kid by the hand of his friend the Adullamite, to receive his pledge from the woman's hand: but he found her not.

21: Then he asked the men of that place, saying, Where is the harlot, that was openly by the way side? And they said, There was no harlot in this place.

22: And he returned to Judah, and said, I cannot find her; and also the men of the place said, that there was no harlot in this place.

23: And Judah said, Let her take it to

her, lest we be shamed: behold, I sent this kid, and thou hast not found her.

24: And it came to pass about three months after, that it was told Judah, saying, Tamar thy daughter in law hath played the harlot; and also, behold, she is with child by whoredom. And Judah said, Bring her forth, and let her be burnt.

25: When she was brought forth, she sent to her father in law, saying, By the man, whose these are, am I with child: and she said, Discern, I pray thee, whose are these, the signet, and bracelets, and staff.

26: And Judah acknowledged them, and said, She hath been more righteous than I; because that I gave her not to Shelah my son. And he knew her again no more.

27: And it came to pass in the time of her travail, that, behold, twins were in her womb.

In the Gospel Of Mark, we find another case of incest, when we're told that Herod married his brother's wife.

Mark 6:18: For John had said unto Herod, It is not lawful for thee to have thy brother's wife.

We've all heard the story of Adam and Eve and their adventures in the Garden Of Eden, but there's a lot more to the story then our bibles let on. The Book of Genesis was written by Moses, a Hebrew, and an ancient ancestor of the Jews, so it's only logical that if you want to get to the bottom of the story, you need to read what they have to say about it. After all; it's their history, not

ours. I can only imagine why the early church never included the original version of the biblical stories in their doctrine. Perhaps they had a hard enough time trying to make people believe what they'd written in the New Testament, much-less, throwing in the extra added fantasy that the original stories portray as well.

The Dictionary Of Jewish Lore And Legend by Alan Unterman, Thames & Hudson publisher, 1991, is an excellent reference book for learning the origin of the stories and characters found in the bible. Stories that portray a totally different perspective than what the average bible totter has become accustom to, and one, the church will never preach.

The Book Of Genesis which includes the Garden Of Eden adventure written by Moses is a well written documentary of the beginning of time, and the appearance of the human species on our planet. It also includes the arrival of the animal kingdom back in those remote eons of our past. What makes the story so fascinating to me is the fact that Moses wasn't even born until the middle of the Bronze Age, or less than 1,500 years before Jesus Christ. It's beyond amazing that he could have written about the beginning of time which took place approximately 4.5 billion years before he was even born. I guess that makes him a retroprophet of the highest order, and the most astounding author the world has ever known. In my opinion, Moses was a very imaginative, middle eastern, fiction writer (or should I say, the ghost writers who wrote in his name were)?

The following mid eastern fables came from Moses and were passed down orally by the Rabbis to the people; this folklore was, and still is, well-known to people in the middle east but in the time of Constantine The Great, who created Catholicism, these fables were either edited out of the previous Catholic scriptures (Vetus Latina) or only basic references were made to them.

Adam - This was the first human according to Moses. He was made out of the dust taken from the four corners of the earth (the earth was still flat then) and God breathed the breath of life into him on Mount Moriah. The shocking detail of this story is the fact that God created Adam as a hermaphrodite, a combination of male and female with both sets of reproductive organs. Thus; when God made Eve, he simply separated Adam's two physical forms. When Adam was first created he was gigantic in size (made in the image of God) but was reduced to normal human dimensions after he committed the original sin in the Garden of Eden. The mystical book of the Angel Raziel, is said to have been attributed to Adam.

Eve - She was Adam's second wife and considered to be the mother of the human race. Eve was originally joined to Adam back to back, as an Androgyny (being both male and female). The popular Christian belief that the serpent tempted Eve to eat the forbidden fruit is only part of the original story. According to Moses, the author of Genesis, the serpent transformed itself into the physical form of Satan and he and Eve had sexual intercourse; Eve became pregnant and gave birth to Cain.

Cain - If Cain really was Satan's son, then his descendants (Kenites) must have interbreed with other clans and spread Satan's lineage throughout the world (that pretty well explains why the world is like it is today, especially America).

It's possible that Satan had other children besides Cain according to what Jesus said.

Mt:13:38: The field is the world; the good seed are the children of the kingdom; but the tares are the children of the wicked one;

The following verse in 1. John, also reinstates that Cain was the son of the devil.

1Jn:3:12: Not as Cain, who was of that wicked one, and slew his brother. And wherefore slew he him? Because his own works were evil, and his brother's righteous.

Lilith - She was Adam's first wife, but ran away from him because she refused to be dominated by a man. Sound familiar? It was Lilith, who God intended to be the mother of the human race. Lilith is the Demon Queen Of The Night, and denounced the name of God when she could not obtain equal status with Adam. I guess you could say that she was also the founding member of the Women's Liberation Movement. The legend of Lilith seems to come right out of Greek mythology. After Adam, she married Samael (Satan), the master of evil forces. She has long black hair and flies through the night looking for babies to eat and looking for men who sleep alone to have sex with, so she can get pregnant and have more demonic children. Lilith was such an ingrained part of middle eastern folklore that special care was taken to protect children and pregnant mothers from her torment. Amulets were worn as protection and in the case of a women about to give birth, the names of protective angels were written on the door of her nursery, and the room was surrounded with burning coals. Also, it was not safe to drink anything potable from outside during certain times of the year because the blood from Lilith's menstrual flow would fall from the sky as she flew around at night. One more point; Lilith also tried to fool wise old King Solomon and make him think that she was the Queen Of Sheba, but when he saw her hairy legs, he knew right off the bat that something was up because demon queens were known for their hairy legs.

Serpent – Moses's legend of the serpent is an awesome one to say the least. In the Garden Of Eden, the serpent had two legs and walked upright. It could even talk and it ate the same food as Adam and Eve. The serpent used to watch Adam and Eve having sexual intercourse and he became obsessed with Eve and desired some action for himself. At the instigation of Satan, and being possessed by him also, the serpent persuaded Eve to eat the forbidden fruit which lead to them having sexual intercourse.

When God found out what had happened, he cut off the arms and legs of the serpent and cast an everlasting curse on him that caused the serpent to crawl upon the ground.

Gen:3:14: And the LORD God said unto the serpent, Because thou hast done this, thou art cursed above all cattle, and above every beast of the field; upon thy belly shalt thou go, and dust shalt thou eat all the days of thy life:

When the serpent had sexual intercourse with Eve, it ejaculated its demon semen into her which in turn polluted the blood line of her descendants. Moses cleansed the people of Israel from Eve's tainted blood line when he received the Torah from God, at Mount Sinai. However; according to legend, we Gentiles have never been cleansed of the serpent's demon semen.

Interesting enough, Moses erected a brazen serpent on a pole during the Hebrew's forty years of wandering in the desert. It was blessed with magical powers and could heal people who were bitten by snakes. It stood for almost 600 years, until Hezekiah destroyed it during one of his idol smashing binges.

2Kgs:18:4: He removed the

high places, and brake the images, and cut down the groves, and brake in pieces the brasen serpent that Moses had made: for unto those days the children of Israel did burn incense to it: and he called it Nehushtan.

Angel Of Death - It's intriguing to note here that the Angel Of Death, whose gruesome task it is to end human life, originally had the face of a serpent. Though today, we picture him as having a skull's face, a black hood and his famous sickle that he never leaves home without.

Satan - He was the King Of The Demons. Originally; Satan was the greatest of all the angels, and he had twice as many wings as the others but he refused to pay homage to Adam, so God expelled him from heaven. Satan could not bow to a human made out of dust when he himself was a part of the Godhead. Satan has many different names and can take on any physical form that he chooses. He also has a host of fallen angels on his side, and he, and they wander throughout the earth tormenting and tempting men's souls. Satan, had sexual intercourse with Eve and became the father of

Cain. Because of Eve's affair with Satan, the first child born on earth was conceived with demon seed, that means that through her lineage (Eve's family tree), we are all related to the devil. Thus; we are all born into sin! In other words, we all have the devil's DNA; I can't imagine why we Gentiles are never taught theses legendary bible stories in church. Can you?

The Book Of Raziel - Raziel is an angel, one that warns mankind of events that will take pace in the future. His book contains magical secrets which are engraved in sapphire stone. Raziel conveyed the contents of his book to Adam in the Garden Of Eden, but I guess he forgot to warn him about his wife and the serpent having an affair. Legend has it that by keeping a copy of Raziel's book in your house, it will safe guard it from disaster. However; apparently, it does not work on protecting gardens, especially, if they're in Eden.

A long haired image of Jesus Christ is one that is clearly implanted in every Christian's mind, but did Jesus really wear his hair long? The bible teaches otherwise.

1Cor:11:14: Doth not even nature itself teach you, that, if a man have long hair, it is a shame unto him.

1Cor.11:16: But if any man seem to be contentious: we have no such custom and neither have the churches of God.

Look what the bible says about money.

Eccl:10:19: A feast is made for laughter, and wine maketh merry: but money answereth all things.

Prov:23:33: Thine eyes shall behold strange women, and thine heart shall utter perverse things.

Ps:137:9: Happy shall he be, that taketh and dasheth thy little ones against the stones.

Gen:38:9: And Onan knew that the seed should not be his; and it came to pass, when he went in unto his brother's wife, that he spilled it on the ground, lest that he should give seed to his brother.

Lev:21:20: Or crookbackt, or a dwarf, or that hath a blemish in his eye, or be scurvy, or scabbed, or hath his stones broken;

Ex:4:25: Then Zipporah took a sharp stone, and cut off the foreskin of her son, and cast it at his feet, and said, Surely a bloody husband art thou to me.

Ezek:18:6: And hath not eaten upon the mountains, neither hath lifted up his eyes to the idols of the house of Israel , neither hath defiled his neighbour's wife, neither hath come near to a menstruous woman,

The verse below teaches slaves to obey their masters like they would the LORD, with "fear and trembling."

Eph:6:5: Servants, be obedient to them that are your masters according to the flesh, with fear and trembling, in singleness of your heart, as unto Christ;

Josh:23:15: Therefore it shall come to pass, that as all good things are come upon you, which the LORD your God promised you; so shall the LORD bring upon you all evil things, until he have destroyed you from off this good land which the LORD your

God hath given you.

Jer:13:23: Can the Ethiopian change his skin, or the leopard his spots? then may ye also do good, that are accustomed to do evil.

Isa:14:2: And the people shall take them, and bring them to their place: and the house of Israel shall possess them in the land of the LORD for servants and handmaids: and they shall take them captives, whose captives they were; and they shall rule over their oppressors.

Lev:21:9: And the daughter of any priest, if she profane herself by playing the whore, she profaneth her father: she shall be burnt with fire.

In the verse below, the LORD offers David three wishes but he can have only one of them, just like the Genie in the bottle in Aladdin's Lamp.

2Sam:24:12: Go and say unto David, Thus saith the LORD, I offer thee three things; choose thee one of them, that I may do it unto thee.

In the next verse, the earth's rotation was moved backwards, ten degrees on Ahaz's sun dial.

Isa:38:8: Behold, I will bring again the shadow of the degrees, which is gone down in the sun dial of Ahaz, ten degrees backward. So the sun returned ten degrees, by which degrees it was gone down.

Isa:3:4: And I will give children to be their princes, and babes shall rule over them.

Ps:78:49: He cast upon them the fierceness of his anger, wrath, and indignation, and trouble, by sending evil angels among them.

Isa:42:1: Behold my servant, whom I uphold; mine elect, in whom my soul delighteth; I have put my spirit upon him: he shall bring forth judgment to the Gentiles.

Note the verse above: Anyone who is not a Jew, is a Gentile.

Job:19:26: And though after my skin worms destroy this body, yet in my flesh shall I see God:

Isa:34:3: Their slain also shall be cast out, and their stink shall come up out of their carcases, and the mountains shall be melted with their blood.

When the bible was being translated (1604-1611), a homosexual was referred to as being a "dog" as in the verse below.

Deut:23:18: Thou shalt not bring the hire of a whore, or the price of a dog, into the house of the LORD thy God for any vow: for even both these are abomination unto the LORD thy God.

Stoning a person to death (as in the verse below) has been a custom in the middle east ever since monkey's learned how to throw rocks. A 19-year-old woman was stoned to death after she was accused of adultery in Afghanistan, just a few years ago.

Deut:22:21: Then they shall bring out the damsel to the door of her father's house, and the men of her city shall stone her with stones that she die: because she hath wrought folly in Israel, to play the whore in her father's house: so shalt thou put evil away from among you.

Sodomite (below) - one who performs or submits to anal intercourse (sodomy).

2Kgs:23:7: And he brake down the houses of the sodomites, that were by the house of the LORD, where the women wove hangings for the grove.

Lev:18:22 : Thou shalt not lie with mankind, as with womankind: it is abomination.

Deut:14:26 : And thou shalt bestow that money for whatsoever thy soul lusteth after, for oxen, or for sheep, or for wine, or for strong drink, or for whatsoever thy soul desireth: and thou shalt eat there before the LORD thy God, and thou shalt rejoice, thou, and thine household,

Joel:3:3: And they have cast lots for my people; and have given a boy for an harlot, and sold a girl for wine, that they might drink.

Isa:23:4: Be thou ashamed, O Zidon: for the sea hath spoken, even the strength of the sea, saying, I travail not, nor bring forth children, neither do I nourish up young men, nor bring up virgins.

Isa:42:8: I am the LORD: that is my name: and my glory will I not give to another, neither my praise to graven images. Note: So Jesus is really not equal to God in glory, according to Isaiah.

Isa:43:11: I, even I, am the LORD; and beside me there is no saviour. Note (above): So who appointed Jesus as the Savior?

Gal:6:13: For neither they themselves who are circumcised keep the law; but desire to have you circumcised, that they may glory in your flesh.

Ezek:23:10: These discovered her nakedness: they took her sons and her daughters, and slew her with the sword: and she became famous among women; for they had executed judgment upon her.

Isa:3:12: As for my people, children are their oppressors, and women rule over them. O my people, they which lead thee cause thee to err, and destroy the way of thy paths.

Gen:38:24: And it came to pass about three months after, that it was told Judah , saying, Tamar thy daughter in law hath played the harlot; and also, behold, she is with child by whoredom. And Judah said, Bring her forth, and let her be burnt.

Jude:1:7: Even as Sodom and Gomorrha, and the cities about them in like manner, giving themselves over to fornication, and going after strange flesh, are set forth for an example, suffering the vengeance of eternal fire.

The following five verses point out the act of having sexual intercourse with pagan idols.

Jer:3:9: And it came to pass through the lightness of her whoredom, that she defiled the land, and committed adultery with stones and with stocks.

Ezek:23:37: That they have committed adultery, and blood is in their hands, and with their idols have they committed adultery, and have also caused their sons, whom they bare unto me, to pass for them through the fire, to devour them.

Ezek:16:17: Thou hast also taken thy fair jewels of my gold and of my silver, which I had given thee, and madest to thyself images of men, and didst commit whoredom with them,

Ezek:16:36: Thus saith the Lord GOD; Because thy filthiness was poured out, and thy nakedness discovered through thy whoredoms with thy lovers, and with all the idols of thy abominations, and by the blood of thy children, which thou didst give unto them;

Ezek:23:7: Thus she committed her whoredoms with them, with all them that were the chosen men of Assyria, and with all on whom she doted: with all their idols she defiled herself.

Ezek:16:25: Thou hast built thy high place at every head of the way, and hast made thy beauty to be abhorred, and hast opened thy feet to every one that passed by, and multiplied thy whoredoms.

Ezek:23:20: For she doted upon their paramours, whose flesh is as the flesh of asses, and whose issue is like the issue of horses.

Note (above): A paramour is a lover.

Isa:66:17: They that sanctify themselves, and purify themselves in the gardens behind one tree in the midst, eating swine's flesh, and the abomination, and the mouse, shall be consumed together, saith the LORD.

Isa:13:5: They come from a far country, from the end of heaven, even the LORD, and the weapons of his indignation, to destroy the whole land.

Zech:11:9: Then said I, I will not feed you: that that dieth, let it die; and that that is to be cut off, let it be cut off; and let the rest eat every one the flesh of another.

Song:1:5: I am black, but comely, O ye daughters of Jerusalem , as the tents of Kedar, as the curtains of Solomon.

Gal:4:23: But he who was of the bondwoman was born after the flesh; but he of the freewoman was by promise.

Lev:19:20: And whosoever lieth carnally with a woman, that is a bondmaid, betrothed to an husband, and not at all redeemed, nor freedom given her; she shall be scourged; they shall not be put to death, because she was not free.

1Sam:11:7: And he took a yoke of oxen, and hewed them in pieces, and sent them throughout all the coasts of Israel by the hands of messengers, saying, Whosoever cometh not forth after Saul and after Samuel, so shall it be done unto his oxen. And the fear of the LORD fell on the people, and they came out with one consent.

Ezek:24:10: Heap on wood, kindle the fire, consume the flesh, and spice it well, and let the bones be burned.

Zech:14:12: And this shall be the plague wherewith the LORD will smite all the people that have fought against Jerusalem; Their flesh shall consume away while they stand upon their feet, and their eyes shall consume away in their holes, and their tongue shall consume away in their mouth.

2Sam:4:7: For when they came into the house, he lay on his bed in his bedchamber, and they smote him, and slew him, and beheaded him, and took his head, and gat them away through the plain all night.

Ex:15:3: The LORD is a man of war: the LORD is his name.

2Sam:4:12: And David commanded his young men, and they slew them, and cut off their hands and their feet, and hanged them up over the pool in Hebron. But they took the head of Ishbosheth, and buried it in the sepulchre of Abner in Hebron.

Ps:22:16: For dogs have compassed me: the assembly of the wicked have inclosed me: they pierced my hands and my feet.

Num:12:12: Let her not be as one dead, of whom the flesh is half consumed when he cometh out of his mother's womb.

Jer:4:7: The lion is come up from his thicket, and the destroyer of the Gentiles is on his way; he is gone forth from his place to make thy land desolate; and thy cities shall be laid waste, without an inhabitant.

1Kgs:2:5: Moreover thou knowest also what Joab the son of Zeruiah did to me, and what he did to the two captains of the hosts of Israel, unto Abner the son of Ner, and unto Amasa the son of Jether, whom he slew, and shed the blood of war in peace, and put the blood of war upon his girdle that was about his loins, and in his shoes that were on his feet.

Deut:12:31: Thou shalt not do so unto the LORD thy God: for every abomination to the LORD, which he hateth, have they done unto their gods; for even their sons and their daughters they have burnt in the fire to their gods.

Deut:23:17: There shall be no whore of the daughters of Israel ,nor a sodomite of the sons of Israel.

2Kgs:21:12: Therefore thus saith the LORD God of Israel , Behold, I am bringing such evil upon Jerusalem and Judah, that whosoever heareth of it, both his ears shall tingle.

Bizarre Verses

Prov:20:8: A king that sitteth in the throne of judgment scattereth away all evil with his eyes.

1Kgs:21:21: Behold, I will bring evil upon thee, and will take away thy posterity, and will cut off from Ahab him that pisseth against the wall, and him that is shut up and left in Israel,

1Kgs:14:10: Therefore, behold, I will bring evil upon the house of Jeroboam, and will cut off from Jeroboam him that pisseth against the wall, and him that is shut up and left in Israel , and will take away the remnant of the house of Jeroboam, as a man taketh away dung, till it be all gone.

2Sam:12:11: Thus saith the LORD, Behold, I will raise up evil against thee out of thine own house, and I will take thy wives before thine eyes, and give them unto thy neighbour, and he shall lie with thy wives in the sight of this sun.

1Sam:16:14: But the Spirit of the LORD departed from Saul, and an evil spirit from the LORD troubled him.

Isa:22:13: And behold joy and gladness, slaying oxen, and killing sheep, eating flesh, and drinking wine: let us eat and drink; for to morrow we shall die.

Dan:8:24: And his power shall be mighty, but not by his own power: and he shall destroy wonderfully, and shall prosper, and practise, and shall destroy the mighty and the holy people.

Ps:58:10: The righteous shall rejoice when he seeth the vengeance: he shall wash his feet in the blood of the wicked.

Deut:28:56: The tender and delicate woman among you, which would not adventure to set the sole of her foot upon the ground for delicateness and tenderness, her eye shall be evil toward the husband of her bosom, and toward her son, and toward her daughter,

Deut:28:54: So that the man that is tender among you, and very delicate, his eye shall be evil toward his brother, and toward the wife of his bosom, and toward the remnant of his children which he shall leave:

Prov:5:5: Her feet go down to death; her steps take hold on hell.

Bizarre Verses

Ps:139:8: If I ascend up into heaven, thou art there: if I make my bed in hell, behold, thou art there.

Prov: 6:13: He winketh with his eyes, he speaketh with his feet, he teacheth with his fingers;

Deut:22:14: And give occasions of speech against her, and bring up an evil name upon her, and say, I took this woman, and when I came to her, I found her not a maid:

Isa: 3:18 : In that day the Lord will take away the bravery of their tinkling ornaments about their feet, and their cauls, and their round tires like the moon,

Deut:17:12: And the man that will do presumptuously, and will not hearken unto the priest that standeth to minister there before the LORD thy God, or unto the judge, even that man shall die: and thou shalt put away the evil from Israel.

Deut:15:9: Beware that there be not a thought in thy wicked heart, saying, The seventh year, the year of release, is at hand; and thine eye be evil against thy poor brother, and thou givest him nought; and he cry unto the LORD against thee, and it be sin unto thee.

Lev:15:17: And every garment, and every skin, whereon is the seed of copulation, shall be washed with water, and be unclean until the even.

Lev:15:16: And if any man's seed of copulation go out from him, then he shall wash all his flesh in water, and be unclean until the even.

Lev:15:19: And if a woman have an issue, and her issue in her flesh be blood, she shall be put apart seven days: and whosoever toucheth her shall be unclean until the even.

Hab:2:16: Thou art filled with shame for glory: drink thou also, and let thy foreskin be uncovered: the cup of the LORD's right hand shall be turned unto thee, and shameful spewing shall be on thy glory.

Song:7:1: How beautiful are thy feet with shoes, O prince's daughter! the joints of thy thighs are like jewels, the work of the hands of a cunning workman.

Isa:3:16: Moreover the LORD saith, Because the daughters of Zion are haughty, and walk with stretched forth necks and wanton eyes, walking and mincing as they go, and making a tinkling with their feet:

Job:3:12: Why did the knees prevent me? or why the breasts that I should suck?

Job:21:24: His breasts are full of milk, and his bones are moistened with marrow.

Num:11:12: Have I conceived all this people? have I begotten them, that thou shouldest say unto me, Carry them in thy bosom, as a nursing father beareth the sucking child, unto the land which thou swarest unto their fathers?

Prov:5:19: Let her be as the loving hind and pleasant roe; let her breasts satisfy thee at all times; and be thou ravished always with her love.

Song:4:5: Thy two breasts are like two young roes that are twins, which feed among the lilies.

Song:8:10: I am a wall, and my breasts like towers: then was I in his eyes as one that found favour.

Isa:66:11: That ye may suck, and be satisfied with the breasts of her consolations; that ye may milk out, and be delighted with the abundance of her glory.

Ezek:23:34: Thou shalt even drink it and suck it out, and thou shalt break the sherds thereof, and pluck off thine own breasts: for I have spoken it, saith the Lord GOD.

Isa:24:6: Therefore hath the curse devoured the earth, and they that dwell therein are desolate: therefore the inhabitants of the earth are burned, and few men left.

Isa:14:12: How art thou fallen from heaven, O Lucifer, son of the morning! how art thou cut down to the ground, which didst weaken the nations!

Jer:22:19: He shall be buried with the burial of an ass, drawn and cast forth beyond the gates of Jerusalem.

Hosea:9:14: Give them, O LORD: what wilt thou give? give them a miscarrying womb and dry breasts.

Lk:14:26: If any man come to me, and hate not his father, and mother, and wife, and children, and brethren, and sisters, yea, and his own life also, he cannot be my disciple.

Mt:5:30: And if thy right hand offend thee, cut it off, and cast it from thee: for it is profitable for thee that one of thy members should perish, and not that thy whole body should be cast into hell.

Mk:9:1: And he said unto them, Verily I say unto you, That there be some of them that stand here, which shall not taste of death, till they have seen the kingdom of God come with power.

Acts:12:23: And immediately the angel of the Lord smote him, because he gave not God the glory: and he was eaten of worms, and gave up the ghost.

Jn:11:39: Jesus said, Take ye away the stone. Martha, the sister of him that was dead, saith unto him, Lord, by this time he stinketh: for he hath been dead four days.

Song:8:8: We have a little sister, and she hath no breasts: what shall we do for our sister in the day when she shall be spoken for?

Prov:13:24: He that spareth his rod hateth his son: but he that loveth him chasteneth him betimes.

Hab:2:15: Woe unto him that giveth his neighbour drink, that puttest thy bottle to him, and makest him drunken also, that thou mayest look on their nakedness!

Isa:65:8: Thus saith the LORD, As the new wine is found in the cluster, and one saith, Destroy it not; for a blessing is in it: so will I do for my servants' sakes, that I may not destroy them all.

Ex:31:14: Ye shall keep the sabbath therefore; for it is holy unto you: every one that defileth it shall surely be put to death: for whosoever doeth any work therein, that soul shall be cut off from among his people.

Note: It must be pointed out here that the Sabbath is from Friday evening, until Saturday evening, not on Sunday as Christians have been led to believe.

Rv:1:18: I am he that liveth, and was dead; and, behold, I am alive for evermore, Amen; and have the keys of hell and of death.

Zech:9:6: And a bastard shall dwell in Ashdod, and I will cut off the pride of the Philistines.

1Chron:20:3: And he brought out the people that were in it, and cut them with saws, and with harrows of iron, and with axes. Even so dealt David with all the cities of the children of Ammon. And David and all the people returned to Jerusalem.

Jer:51:22: With thee also will I break in pieces man and woman; and with thee will I break in pieces old and young; and with thee will I break in pieces the young man and the maid;

Ps:68:23: That thy foot may be dipped in the blood of thine enemies, and the tongue of thy dogs in the same.

Rv:19:13: And he was clothed with a vesture dipped in blood: and his name is called The Word of God.

Lk:13:1: There were present at that season some that told him of the Galilaeans, whose blood Pilate had mingled with their sacrifices.

Isa:66:17: They that sanctify themselves, and purify themselves in the gardens behind one tree in the midst, eating swine's flesh, and the abomination, and the mouse, shall be consumed together, saith the LORD.

Mal:2:3: Behold, I will corrupt your seed, and spread dung upon your faces, even the dung of your solemn feasts; and one shall take you away with it.

Ezek:4:12: And thou shalt eat it as barley cakes, and thou shalt bake it with dung that cometh out of man, in their sight.

Ezek:4:15: Then he said unto me, Lo, I have given thee cow's dung for man's dung, and thou shalt prepare thy bread therewith.

Ezek:5:10: Therefore the fathers shall eat the sons in the midst of thee, and the sons shall eat their fathers; and I will execute judgments in thee, and the whole remnant of thee will I scatter into all the winds.

Lev:2:13: And every oblation of thy meat offering shalt thou season with salt; neither shalt thou suffer the salt of the covenant of thy God to be lacking from thy meat offering: with all thine offerings thou shalt offer salt.

Hosea:13:4: Yet I am the LORD thy God from the land of Egypt , and thou shalt know no god but me: for there is no saviour beside me.

2Sam:10:4: Wherefore Hanun took David's servants, and shaved off the one half of their beards, and cut off their garments in the middle, even to their buttocks, and sent them away.

Lev:20:13: If a man also lie with mankind, as he lieth with a woman, both of them have committed an abomination: they shall surely be put to death; their blood shall be upon them.

Lev:20:14: And if a man take a wife and her mother, it is wickedness: they shall be burnt with fire, both he and they; that there be no wickedness among you. Lev:20:15: And if a man lie with a beast, he shall surely be put to death: and ye shall slay the beast.

Lev:20:16: And if a woman approach unto any beast, and lie down thereto, thou shalt kill the woman, and the beast: they shall surely be put to death; their blood shall be upon them.

Jer:44:17: But we will certainly do whatsoever thing goeth forth out of our own mouth, to burn incense unto the queen of heaven, and to pour out drink offerings unto her, as we have done, we, and our fathers, our kings, and our princes, in the cities of Judah, and in the streets of Jerusalem: for then had we plenty of victuals, and were well, and saw no evil.

Job:21:14: Therefore they say unto God, Depart from us; for we desire not the knowledge of thy ways.

Josh:23:15: Therefore it shall come to pass, that as all good things are come upon you, which the LORD your God promised you; so shall the LORD bring upon you all evil things, until he have destroyed you from off this good land which the LORD your God hath given you.

Isa:45:7: I form the light, and create darkness: I make peace, and create evil: I the LORD do all these things.

Micah:7:17: They shall lick the dust like a serpent, they shall move out of their holes like worms of the earth: they shall be afraid of the LORD our God, and shall fear because of thee.

Job:24:21: He evil entreateth the barren that beareth not: and doeth not good to the widow.

Ps:77:9: Hath God forgotten to be gracious? hath he in anger shut up his tender mercies? Selah.

Deut:14:1: Ye are the children of the LORD your God: ye shall not cut yourselves, nor make any baldness between your eyes for the dead.

Hosea:1:9: Then said God, Call his name Lo-ammi: for ye are not my people, and I will not be your God.

Ps:58:10: The righteous shall rejoice when he seeth the vengeance: he shall wash his feet in the blood of the wicked.

2Kgs:3:27: Then he took his eldest son that should have reigned in his stead, and offered him for a burnt offering upon the wall. And there was great indignation against Israel : and they departed from him, and returned to their own land.

Rom:7:15: For that which I do I allow not: for what I would, that do I not; but what I hate, that do I.

Ex:18:19: Hearken now unto my voice, I will give thee counsel, and God shall be with thee: Be thou for the people to Godward, that thou mayest bring the causes unto God:

Jn:12:24: Verily, verily, I say unto you, Except a corn of wheat fall into the ground and die, it abideth alone: but if it die, it bringeth forth much fruit.

Jer:33:5: They come to fight with the Chaldeans, but it is fill them with the dead bodies of men, whom I have slain in mine anger and in my fury, and for all whose wickedness I have hid my face from this city.

Hosea:11:9: I will not execute the fierceness of mine anger, I will not return to destroy Ephraim: for I am God, and not man; the Holy One in the midst of thee: and I will not enter into the city.

Jer:48:10: Cursed be he that doeth the work of the LORD deceitfully, and cursed be he that keepeth back his sword from blood.

1Kgs:13:2: And he cried against the altar in the word of the LORD, and said, O altar, altar, thus saith the LORD; Behold, a child shall be born unto the house of David, Josiah by name; and upon thee shall he offer the priests of the high places that burn incense upon thee, and men's bones shall be burnt upon thee.

2Kgs:17:31: And the Avites made Nibhaz and Tartak, and the Sepharvites burnt their children in fire to Adrammelech and Anammelech, the gods of Sepharvaim.

2Chron:34:5: And he burnt the bones of the priests upon their altars, and cleansed Judah and Jerusalem.

Nahum:3:6: And I will cast abominable filth upon thee, and make thee vile, and will set thee as a gazingstock.

Ezek:32:4: Then will I leave thee upon the land, I will cast thee forth upon the open field, and will cause all the fowls of the heaven to remain upon thee, and I will fill the beasts of the whole earth with thee.

2Sam:20:12: And Amasa wallowed in blood in the midst of the highway. And when the man saw that all the people stood still, he removed Amasa out of the highway into the field, and cast a cloth upon him, when he saw that every one that came by him stood still.

2Sam:20:22: Then the woman went unto all the people in her wisdom. And they cut off the head of Sheba the son of Bichri, and cast it out to Joab. And he blew a trumpet, and they retired from the city, every man to his tent. And Joab returned to Jerusalem unto the king.

Ex:32:20: And he took the calf which they had made, and burnt it in the fire, and ground it to powder, and strawed it upon the water, and made the children of Israel drink of it.

The next two verses teach slave masters how

to mark their slaves with an "aul." In case you didn't know, an "aul" is a tool that looks like an ice pick.

Deut:15:17: Then thou shalt take an aul, and thrust it through his ear unto the door, and he shall be thy servant for ever. And also unto thy maidservant thou shalt do likewise.

Ex:21:6: Then his master shall bring him unto the judges; he shall also bring him to the door, or unto the door post; and his master shall bore his ear through with an aul; and he shall serve him for ever.

Ps:57:4: My soul is among lions: and I lie even among them that are set on fire, even the sons of men, whose teeth are spears and arrows, and their tongue a sharp sword.

2Kings:6:25: And there was a great famine in Samaria: and, behold, they besieged it, until an ass's head was sold for fourscore pieces of silver, and the fourth part of a cab of dove's dung for five pieces of silver.

This is all of the space allotted for this topic at this time, however; the list is far from being complete. More Bizarre Verses in: Vol. 2.

The story of the messiah coming in the sky (Revelation Of Jesus Christ) was originally written about in the Book Of Enoch. The Book of Enoch was written before the great flood and the messiah still hasn't shown up. Enoch's book never made it into any of the bibles because it was deemed uninspired by God.

Jude:1:14: And Enoch also, the seventh from Adam, prophesied of these, saying, Behold, the Lord cometh with ten thousands of his saints.

Jude:1:15: to execute judgment upon all, and to convince all that are ungodly among them of all their ungodly deeds which they have ungodly committed, and to all their hard speeches which ungodly sinners have spoken against him.

Saint John The Divine, who wrote The Revelation of Jesus Christ, did his own version of Enoch's story of the coming messiah. St. John also borrowed bits and pieces from the prophets of the Old Testament (who also wrote their own revelation) and of course, St. John also borrowed from what Jesus taught. Scholars now know beyond a shadow of a doubt that St. John's Book of Revelation was originally started in the year 90 C.E. but was added to, and edited by at least seven other ghost writers up until 290 A.D., some 200 years after it was started. Since Rome destroyed the last Jewish temple in the year 70 C.E., and Constantine The Great legalized Christianity in around the year 310 AD., it makes me suspicious that perhaps Rome had a bigger hand in creating the New Testament then recorded history lets on.

The story of the messiah coming to judge the world depends on the reader's ignorance of biblical history to exert its initial effect, which is to drive people into religious psychosis and theological paranoia. It's a shame that our own government used these same psychological tactics to control the masses here in America, and they still do!

If each individual person would do their own in depth study of history and of the bible, they would realize what a science fiction fantasy, this mid eastern fairy tale really is.

The following three verses point out how the threat of Judgment Day evolved throughout biblical history and how it was updated each time it failed to occur.

Book Of Enoch (seven generations after Adam and Eve).

Jude 1:14: And Enoch also, the seventh from Adam, prophesied of these, saying, Behold, the Lord cometh with ten thousands of his saints.

Book of Haggai (approximately 500 years before Jesus).

Hag:2:6: For thus saith the LORD of hosts; Yet once, it is a little while, and I will shake the heavens, and the earth, and the sea, and the dry land;

Book Of Revelation (written 90 C.E. To 290 A.D.).

Rv:1:3: Blessed is he that readeth, and they that hear the words of this prophecy, and keep those things which are written therein: for the time is at hand.

The idea that these are the last days is a hoax that gets played out every time something traumatic happens in history. Religious fanatics claimed that it was the last days during the Revolutionary War; the War Of 1812, the Mexican American War, the Civil War, World War 1, World War 2, Korean War,Vietnam

War, Iraqi War and then again at the turn of the millennium (Y2K). The last time they played the last days card was in December 2012, when the Aztec calendar was coming to an end - but we're still here, and still no sign of the Messiah. Religious fanatics are so hung up on the last days hoax that now it's more of a curse than a prophecy, it appears as if they want something catastrophic to happen to mankind (talk about a false prophet).

With history as a reference, it's quite clear that these are the most beneficial of days in recorded history, not the last days. With the advancement of modern science and technology, people are living longer and living life to its fullest; whereas a hundred years ago people suffered in pain and emotional trauma, and died very young due to common illnesses. The human experience is in its infancy and life is evolving for the better every day, peace and love are obtainable, it all starts in your mind, change the way you think and your actions will follow suit. If enough people join in, eventually, "the world will be as one," John Lennon (The Beatles).

Pg. 136   Closing Statement

The Catholics had the bible (Latin Vulgate) for over a thousand years before the Protestant, English Bible was published. During that time, Catholicism spread across Europe by the Holy Roman Empire. Anyone who did not submit to the will of the church was charged with heresy and burnt alive at the stake and their property confiscated. Millions of the people who were executed by the church were peace-loving gypsies and innocent, nature worshiping villagers (many of them were our ancestors).

2Thes:1:8: In flaming fire taking vengeance on them that know not God, and that obey not the gospel of our Lord Jesus Christ:

When the Spaniards spread Catholicism, they sailed for the Americas searching for gold and spices but forcefully conquered and converted the indigenous people they encountered. The Aztec Empire (Mexico) was virtually wiped-out in 1521 by Hernando Cortes and his bloody band of conquistadors.

2Chron:15:13: That whosoever would not seek the LORD God of Israel should be put to death, whether small or great, whether man or woman.

When the English colonized the New World, they had their own version of the scriptures and used them to justify bringing African tribesmen and women to North America as slaves.

Lev:25:44: Both thy bondmen, and thy bondmaids, which thou shalt have, shall be of the heathen that are round about you; of them shall ye buy bondmen and bondmaids.

Settlers who spread west across America justified annihilating the North American Indians by what they read in the English Bible.

Psalms:44:2: How thou didst drive out the heathen with thy hand, and plantedst them; how thou didst afflict the people, and cast them out.

This is how the word of God came down to us today (in a blood bath), it wasn't brought here on the wings of a dove by sweet Jesus, nor his disciples (apostles).

This book has been written to expose the bible's negative influence on American history and how the Holy Scriptures misled millions of faithful followers into believing that they were a superior race, giving rise to racial supremacy and prejudice in America.

Psalms:18:43: Thou hast delivered me from the strivings of the people; and thou hast made me the head of the heathen: a people whom I have not known shall serve me.

The entire bible (scriptures) took place in the middle east and it's an historical record of their customs, culture(s), mythology, perception of God and so on. So why in the world would anybody in their right mind want to establish a country in the western hemisphere such as America, and base it on the same dogmatic principles found in the middle east? I will explain this turn of events in:

That Can't Be In The Bible Vol. 2.

God is real but the human consciousness has not evolved far enough yet to be able to comprehend or perceive who, where or what God is. The spirit of God is all around us and can be felt (sensed) if one has a clear mind and can tune in with it, when one does, it's a natural high!

Made in the USA
Columbia, SC
21 October 2020

23257802R10083